Buildings + Projects

rob wellington quigley

rob wellington quigley

Buildings + Projects

Introduction by
Magali Sarfatti Larson
Essays by
Michael Benedikt
Aaron Betsky
Ann Jarmusch

Buildings + Projects

rob wellington quigley

Contents

First published in the United States of America in 1996 by
Rizzoli International Publications, Inc.
300 Park Avenue South, New York NY 10010

Library of Congress Cataloging-in-Publication Data

Quigley, Rob Wellington.
    Rob Wellington Quigley : buildings and projects / introduction by
Magali Sarfatti Larson ; essays by Michael Benedikt ... [et al.].
        p.   cm.
    Includes bibliographical references.
    ISBN 0–8478–1945–0 (HC). — ISBN 0–8478–1946–9 (PB)
    1. Quigley, Rob Wellington—Themes, motives. 2. Architecture,
Modern—20th century—California, Southern.   I. Benedikt, Michael.
II. Title.
NA737.Q54A4   1996   95–43747
720'.92—dc20   CIP

Designed by Tenazas Design, San Francisco

Cover and contents page photograph: 202 Island Inn, San Diego, 1992
Frontispiece: Palm tree detail, Beaumont Building, San Diego, 1988

Printed and bound in Hong Kong

acknowledgments

Writers, critics, and even architects like myself would have you believe that efforts such as those illustrated in this book are the work of a single mind and hand.

There is good reason for this. It is hard enough to communicate the complex content of architecture without attempting simultaneously to explain the reality of co-authorship inherent in the art of architecture. I find the practice of architecture is in fact a rich and fascinating collaboration, not only with our clients but with the enormously talented people who work with us.

Architecture is distinguished from the fine arts not just because of its public utility, but because of the collaborative nature of the creative process.

To that end, the most important pages in this book are the last three.

Rob Quigley

What we call architecture

emerged from the Italian Renaissance as one of the arts recently ennobled by powerful and sophisticated patrons. Throughout the subsequent long transformation of European societies, architects endeavored to maintain their social identity as artists and chief makers of architecture, even into the nineteenth century, when they strove to follow the modern path of professionalization. Architects were relatively more successful than painters, sculptors, or musicians in merging their art with the professional organization and delivery of services. Yet architecture's relation to art makes it unusual among established professions: it claims legitimacy from its artistic lineage, yet in our society it is both difficult and puzzling to assert expertise in aesthetic domains. Special among professions, architecture is something of a paradox among the arts.

Architecture inhabits a special art world not strictly comparable to that of other arts that operate directly in their special markets. From the late seventeenth century on, markets for unique art objects (among which easel paintings are the quintessential example) appeared in major European cities and continued to expand with the rise of an affluent class of urban bourgeois. While representations of architecture could circulate as drawings, single or in textbooks, built architecture could

Introduction

An appropriately f r a g i l e

neither enter the market nor circulate within it. Architecture is unmovable, and in principle more permanent than other art forms.

Yet fixity is only part of what makes architectural objects special. Designers cannot realize their objects first, then attempt to place them in the proper distribution system, as a sculptor approaches art dealers with a new piece of work or a composer presents the score of a concerto to a music director or an impresario. Architects do not "build" their works; to say that is to speak in metaphor. Realizing architectural designs is a collective project that now requires ever more specialized teams of consultants and complex construction crews. While today's architects in the United States summon the consultants, the executants are organized and supervised by contractors and construction managers. But even Renaissance architects were *not* the makers of what they designed. For this they depended on the considerable skills of carpenters, masons, and other tradespeople.

More significantly, architects seldom are the sole creators of (or even less often, solely responsible for) their designs. Normally architects translate clients' needs and desires into an artifact that must obey primordial physical laws as well as satisfy social functions and expectations. It is not frequent, although becoming more so, that architects, acting as their own clients, place a finished building on the market to wait for an unknown buyer. In the large majority of cases, architects work for known clients. They may complain about this dependence, but it is almost inevitable: clients and their programs are sine qua non conditions of existence, simultaneously enabling and constraining the design, shaping architecture and its meaning.

The paradox becomes clear: architecture is an art in which those who claim authorship do not make the object in its final form; it is a collective project in which one player, the designer, often believes in his or her own charismatic authority yet is subject to the client's legal and financial control; it is a contemporary art that still exists under relations akin to those of ancient patronage rather than the modern market; and I would contend that it is an art whose meaning depends as much on external constraints as on the architect's free creative expression. Also, these art objects so intimately dependent on the existence and will of a client often are intended not for the client him or herself, but for the users.

In our capitalist societies, dominated by principles of utility and efficiency, art is considered "useless." The Frankfurt School theorists Theodor Adorno and Max Horkheimer noted that this uselessness was precisely the utility of art. The existence of a domain free from the principle of utility attests that our society does not destroy but, on the contrary, preserves those values that it holds both opposite and subordinate to its central tenets: beauty is subordinate to utility, sentiment to business, feeling to calculation, enjoyment to work, art to industry, disinterest to interest; and, more broadly, the irrational is subordinate to the rational, the spiritual to the material, the feminine to the masculine. Useless, superfluous art indeed lives

"apart from the sphere of our sorrow,"

as the poet Shelley wrote.

But not architecture. Before being beautiful, most buildings are useful: they are not separate from the process of life, but the stage on which we conduct our lives. In architecture, these paired values are not opposites but intimately, indissolubly bound together.

Architecture's usefulness—the complexity of this paradox—is precisely what makes it fascinating. It exists as art not because of its alleged creative freedom, but within and because of its constraints; it is not separate from everyday life, but in our midst, almost unnoticeable, not as monument but as background.

Let us see what Rob Quigley makes of this paradox, these constraints, architecture's unique potential.

When I first met Quigley in 1988, he told me how he had come back to California in 1971 after two years with the Peace Corps in Chile. During this time, Salvador Allende and his socialist party had campaigned for the presidency and won; these events and the political environment had a great impact on Quigley. "I went believing I was an artist," he said. "I came back an architect." He went to work for an architecture firm in San Diego and all he heard in the drafting room was: "We could do great work in this firm if we had a great client…" "if it weren't for all those building codes…" "if we just had the budget…." For Quigley, however, "when you start believing that you need a 'patron of the arts' to do good architecture, you are dead." In 1973 he received a commission for a small house, then another; then he put together a small investment group for a four-unit, three-story apartment building and acted as the general contractor ("I wanted to learn from the trades," he explained). That was enough work for him to establish his own firm.

Art

Magali Sarfatti Larson

J Street Inn

When Quigley talks about architecture, he does not talk about form (violated, as the deconstructivists would have it, or otherwise); he does not talk about exquisite details that allow a certain shadow to align at certain times with a certain wall. He talks enthusiastically about a living, lived-in architecture and how it is put together—about the Baltic Inn, for instance. This is the first single room occupancy (SRO) hotel that Quigley built in San Diego, in 1987, with developers Chris Mortenson and Bud Fischer. It is named after the cheapest property on the Monopoly board and has 209 rooms, communal showers on each floor, a lobby, TV room, storage space, and laundry. Built for $3.6 million, it started a wave of SRO construction in California and elsewhere; more than an award-winning building, it became a model and proof that housing affordable to the poorest working people was possible in a for-profit, capitalist environment.

I had seen many pictures of the Baltic Inn, with its clean white facade transfixed by an inverted triangle of ochre-gray stucco that converges on the tall entrance door adorned with the name in neon, but when Quigley finally showed it to me, it took me by surprise. The triangle's virtual summit is above ground; "it emanates from the center, where the heart is," Quigley said, so that on entering the building one should feel central to it, and the building speaks to you. Before starting the next SRO, Quigley interviewed the Inn's residents. They said they missed only one thing: a quiet reading room. The J Street Inn has one; on the other hand, at La Pensione, the laundry room is in the middle of the foot traffic area so that people can meet while doing their wash. Quigley pointed out that the gay yellow and red tiles on the J Street Inn baseboards made them durable and beautiful, and that is what "it" (the architecture) was about: "taking something that has to exist anyway and making it beautiful." Not pretty, not embellished after the fact and dressed up in a false costume—which is what arts patrons often want from their last-minute architects. Beautiful: necessary, durable, and gay.

I once heard a famous European architect explain the architect's task through a notion of duplicity, "having in mind two different goals simultaneously—architecture as autonomous culture, and as the will of the client." Duplicity is not for Rob Quigley. He is able to put emotion in his description of a built-in service wall; he is able to characterize the light that plays back and forth through tall windows in the two-story kitchens of his affordable units in Encinitas as the "luxury" he needs to give them. Quigley's tone when he talks about these projects reminds me of the great Italian poet Eugenio Montale's verse about simple blessings:

"Here even we the poor get our share of riches – it is the scent of lemons."

Sherman Heights Community Center

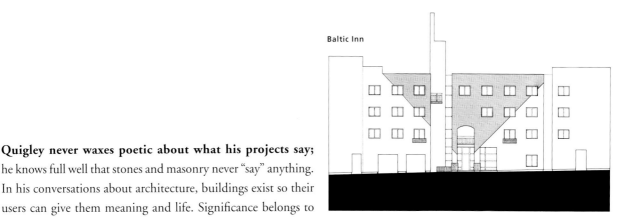

Baltic Inn

Quigley never waxes poetic about what his projects say; he knows full well that stones and masonry never "say" anything. In his conversations about architecture, buildings exist so their users can give them meaning and life. Significance belongs to the living. Quigley is not at all interested in an autonomous architects' culture. He believes that beyond their circle, members of the architecture elite are mute: "The lay person could not care less what architects think," he says.

This does not mean that Rob Quigley does not strive to transcend the mundane aspects of the work he loves. He starts by assuming all of its limitations, to the point that creative expression emanates from that source. The idea of transcendence implicit in his work and words is one he shares with the European modernists of the 1920s: he is not interested in smuggling Art or Form behind the client's back, but in doing architecture. For him, that is a service rendered to those who use his buildings, one that enhances their lives with efficient grace and transcends not the architect's discontent, but life itself.

Rob Quigley, however, talks more simply about seeking a "fit" between architecture and the social ground that nourishes it.

Retreating into the fine arts cannot produce that fit;

on the contrary, he says, it strengthens the popular image of the architect as "someone you call on to make things pretty. An artistic role, but devoid of the substance that distinguishes architecture from decoration." Quigley attempts to find a solution by concentrating resolutely on process, which leads him toward a serious concept of the vernacular. He names the two main ways of making of architecture as "the technical process of construction" and "the social process of design."

Built architecture is local: it does not move, it belongs to a specific place. That is one reason why the universal language of modernism, coarsened, simplified, and transformed into the universal language of corporate capitalism, has erased the sense of a real place from too many of the world's downtowns. Downtown San Diego is a strange mix of this placelessness: ugly and expensive towers, vacant lots, modest industrial buildings, and remnants of what Quigley calls, after historian Kevin Starr, the Arcadian Dream of Southern California.

It is there, between Sixth Avenue and Front Street, between J Street and Market, that Quigley has built three SROs and a more upscale, market-rate apartment complex that occupies a city block. Both this large project and the SRO that won the National AIA Honor Award, 202 Island Inn, break their bulk by modulating their facades in deference to the streets

they face. Like the apartment block, the L-shaped SRO has three different street facades that both serve and project the building's different functions: a hotel, a delightful cafe at the corner, and retail spaces surmounted by the shop owners' rooms on Third Avenue. Here Quigley has forcefully incorporated the dimensions, shapes, and revitalized colors of the old buildings on the block. He does not pretend to ignore this shapeless urban space inhabited by ugly parking structures and expensive apartment towers of reflecting glass. In J Street Inn and 202 Island Inn, a variety of shapes and colors, tightly bound with the functions they serve, suggests how a real cityscape could reconquer that urban emptiness.

To complete the tour of the SROs, there is the considerably more upscale La Pensione in San Diego's Little Italy neighborhood, where Quigley lives and works in the Beaumont Building. Once again, La Pensione is large, but inserted with grace among its low-rise neighbors. It gives strength to the low, Latin-looking walls of the surrounding street, anchoring the scant but still vibrant commercial activity that remains around a freeway built in the 1960s. On one side are La Pensione's two restaurants with sidewalk seating, which look like two buildings—one white and incorporating the facades of a historical building, the other gray stucco—separated by a passageway to a courtyard. Enclosed within four-story-high walls, the courtyard has a tile floor, cafe tables, and a low fountain along the back wall under a planted border and tall, thin cypresses on each side of the windows. The water simply falls out of a tube in the wall, but it plays in the sun and shade, with a clear water sound. It is calm, white, and shady there.

In the Linda Vista Library, the Esperanza Garden Apartments in Encinitas, the Sherman Heights Community Center, the Solana Beach Transit Station, and, of course, in the single-family homes, **Quigley designed directly with the users, following the principle of community design workshops. Small groups facilitated by Quigley and his collaborators actually designed their ideas with the help of colored pasta and crayons.** These design workshops, especially useful for complex or controversial projects, allowed Quigley to resolve the problem of cultural "fit." For some architects, this participatory process would be artistically stifling; for Quigley it has resulted in some of his best work.

But there is more to this idea of finding the fit. There is learning. At Sherman Heights, Quigley learned how Latin Americans see the relationship between concrete and vegetation: the two are not separate, but intimately intertwined. There the garden will grow vertically, the concrete wall will stay raw, and the vines will cover it, growing up to every nook and cranny and getting inside whenever possible. With its porticoes, porches, and verandas, this community center is both civic and residential, domestic and public—a people's house. When an architect listens to learn, he or she escapes the autonomous culture of architectural specialists to enter the living culture of the people who will use the building. Linda Vista's exceptionally well-conceived and beautiful library was Quigley's first public building, and with it he wanted to show what Southern California is really about. Its true vernacular is not based on the pseudo-Mexican architecture and fake adobes adapted from an annexed and dominated people, or on the expediency of late-twentieth-century capitalism, or on the blessed climate and the ocean, but above all on the people who use shopping malls, libraries, and community centers, who need decent housing, and who move, on average, every two years. Starr refers to a sun-drenched mongrel society in California—a synthesis of "Yankee ingenuity and capitalistic skills" and "Latin graciousness and love of life"; but it has not emerged.

Quigley believes that the only way to universal meanings in architecture is through vivid vernaculars. To make an authentic vernacular architecture for an impermanent, multicultural society, he studies and exploits light wood-frame and tilt-up concrete construction technologies. The late California architect Irving Gill used these methods because they responded to the scarcity of local craftsmanship and exploited the immense possibilities afforded by the region's climate. Quigley aspires to do the same. As he writes in his essay "An Architecture of 6 Contradictions" (p. 206), "Over the last few decades, snickers from cold-climate contemporaries have turned to respect and, ironically, emulation as local architects raised raw framing, cheap stucco, and asphalt shingles to an appropriately fragile art. At last, high art and a budget-driven, vernacular reality meet with inspired enthusiasm." Compare this with what an important corporate architect told me in an interview: "The problem of housing…is simply a financial and political responsibility. If society decides to build it, then the architects can do it, but making it cheap is not the answer." This man is wrong. In the Third World, as in the fiercely unequal world of real estate markets in the United States, building cheap must be the answer. To assume civic responsibility, architects like Quigley have to design for meager budgets. Budget constraints compel them to seek architectural beauty where the masters said it was: in shape, mass, and color playing with light.

Johnson House

I visited only one private house designed by Rob Quigley: his own. It is in a five-floor building, a somewhat brutalist, dark-gray stucco structure, too forceful at this time for a neighborhood where Quigley expects an invasion of high rises. It houses the offices of Quigley's firm and of his wife's. They live at the top, in a very large, square living room around a rotunda, which can be closed by folding glass doors but is almost always open. There are bedrooms in the corner towers, narrow stairs to the roof, two stunning pyramids of opaque glass that give light to the lower floors, a concrete fireplace in the exterior wall, and exquisite views of the harbor and the sky. Improbably suspended from earthquake braces in the corner of the living room is a trapeze for the Quigleys' eight-year-old daughter, Thea. On this night, San Diego's starry lights hover around the walls; it is very cool, and there is a fire in the fireplace. The big room wraps itself kindly around the adults who watch the blond child execute very difficult movements on the bar. Attuned to the moment, the setting comes alive with the spontaneous poetry of everyday life.

An appropriately fragile art,

indeed, for a little blue-eyed acrobat who brings the magic of the circus into living rooms.

Mixed-Use Projects

Solana Beach Transit Station

Completed 1995

The Solana Station is a $20 million mixed-use project that eventually will be the new town center for this growing Southern California beach city. The design was created in a series of public workshops and includes a rail station, a large parking garage, retail and restaurant space, low-cost senior housing, artists lofts, and town-house-style apartments. The rail station is now complete; the remainder of the project will be built in phases over eight years.

In a refreshing alternative to development-as-usual, the North County Transit District and the City of Solana Beach consolidated particular properties and interests into a common agenda. Even more courageously, the local residents were asked to define and "design" this politically controversial and complex project.

After a series of orientation workshops, the architects presented the participants with a blank piece of butcher paper. Working in small groups, the community and developers reached a creative consensus on the majority of programmatic items.

The groups expressed concerns about traffic, parking, and design. They wanted this project to become a new community focal point or town center. They stressed establishing a human scale and a comfortable relationship between existing commercial and residential areas. The development had to relate to the railroad tracks while mitigating noise and vibration. In addition, the design had to function with the tracks at grade as well as allow the tracks to be lowered twenty-five feet below grade in the future. Links with Highway 101, an adjacent park, the beach, and the remaining area had to be explored sensitively. The groups also wanted to mask the presence of an 880-space parking garage. A hierarchy was proposed that placed more public retail components near a busy intersection, and quiet residential uses at the north end of the project.

High on the community's list of requests was a design that would be unique and particular to this beach community. The response was design imagery inspired by the World War II-era structures and greenhouse sheds still found throughout the area. The train station acknowledges the vaulted typology of its European origins, but responds more specifically to local traditions. Departing from its self-imposed height limit, the community requested a tower to connote the project's civic importance. The rural-like park around the station is inspired by the nearby sandstone cliffs and beach access stairs. Landscaping in this section will consist only of sparse ground cover and native torrey pine trees.

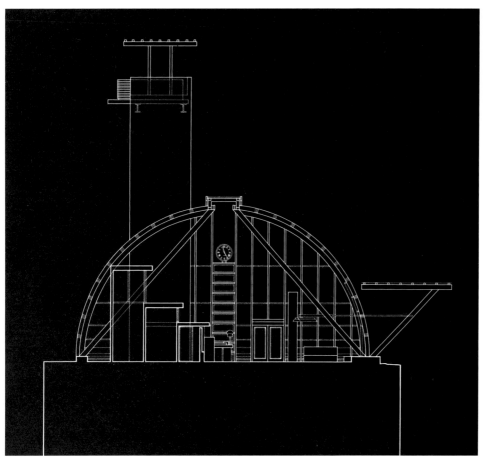

Section

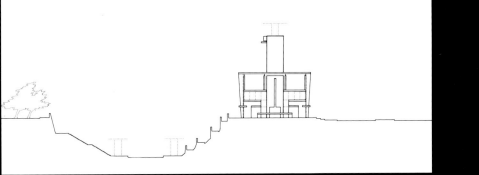

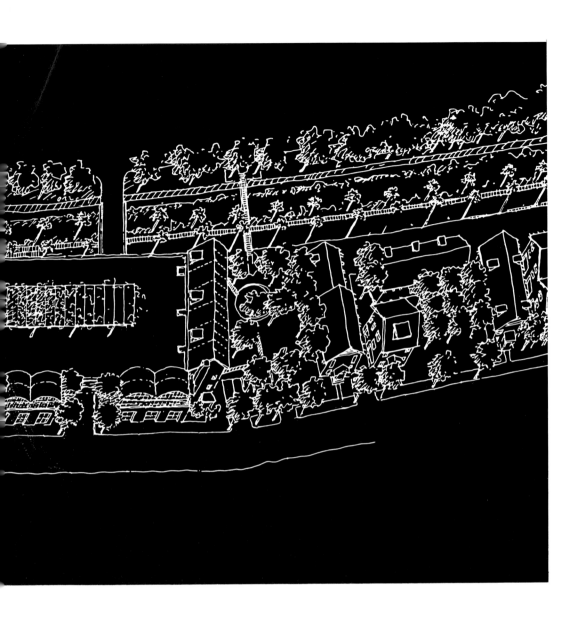

N → Site plan

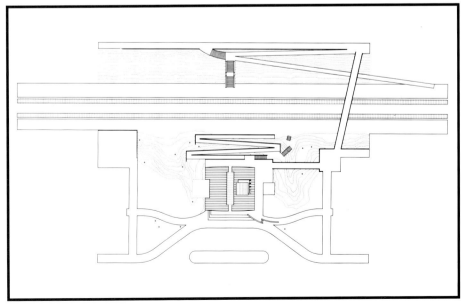

Beaumont Building

Completed 1988

The five-story Beaumont Building sits on a 50' x 50' lot just inside the Little Italy mixed-use/residential area in San Diego. Across the street will eventually stand the northernmost high-density office buildings downtown. The building's ambiguous imagery, neither officelike nor residential, underscores its role as a mediator between these two scales.

The city recently passed laws allowing live/work spaces downtown. The building currently houses a business on the second floor and a business/apartment on the third floor. The fourth and fifth floors contain the owner's office and family home, respectively. The rooftop apartment consists of a series of flexible, unremarkable spaces arranged around a central courtyard, in the Mexican tradition. The open courtyard serves as the apartment's year-round main living space.

The building's forms and shapes respond to bay views, the hot sun, and personal interpretations of San Diego's local architectural heritage. Its dark, unpainted stucco exterior, atypical in this region, reduces both glare and the building's bulk.

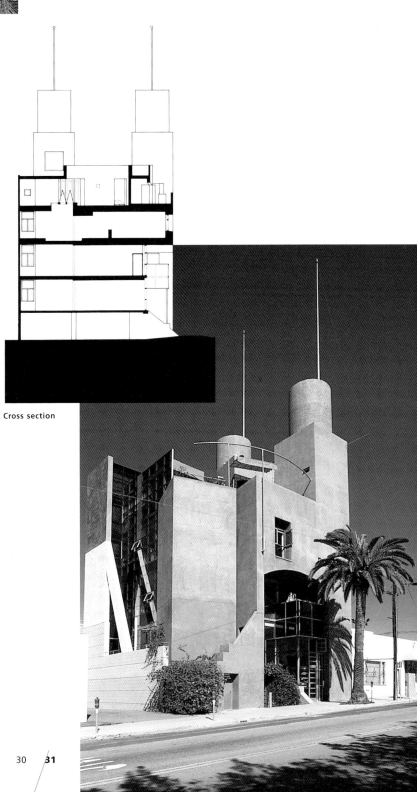

Cross section

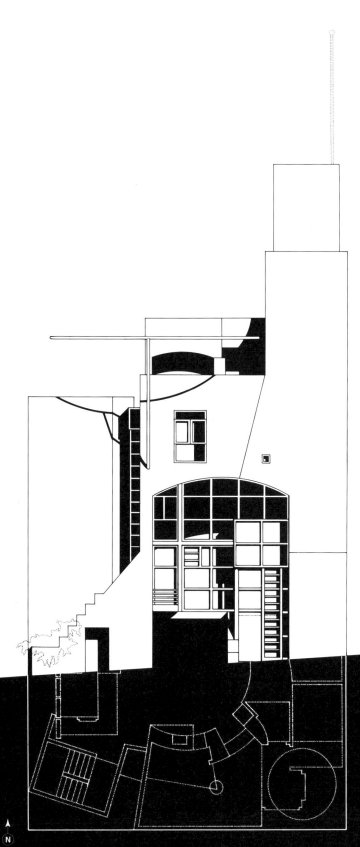

**Front elevation and
partial fifth floor plan**

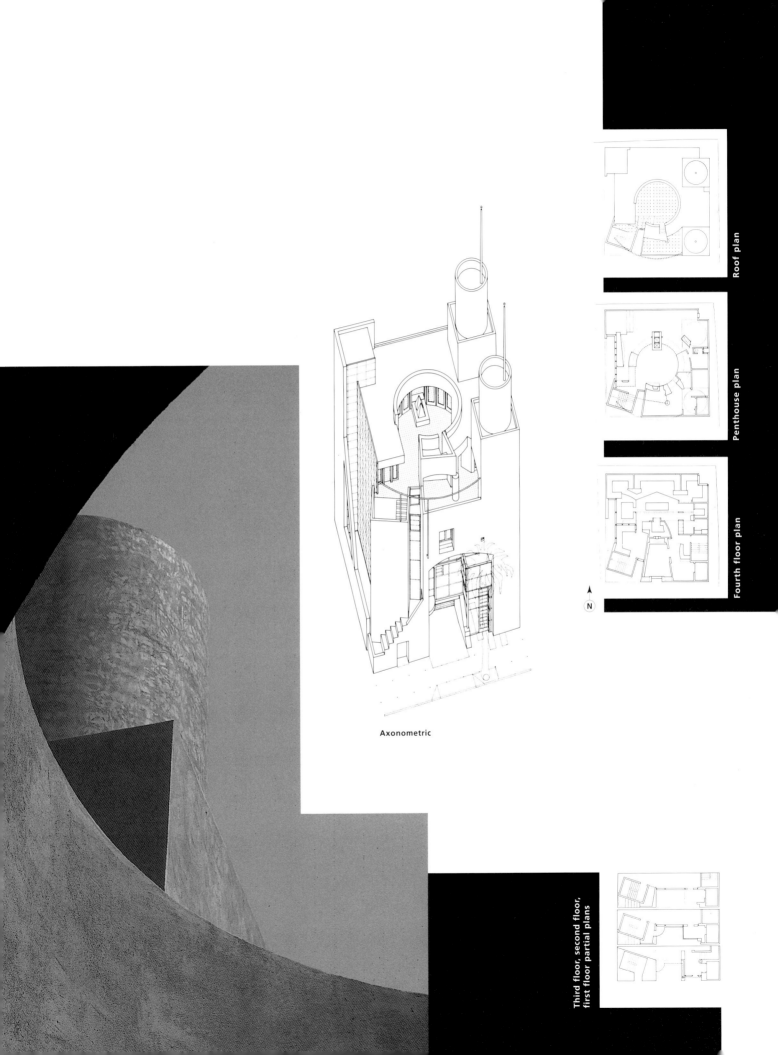

Axonometric

Roof plan

Penthouse plan

Fourth floor plan

N

Third floor, second floor,
first floor partial plans

Foreston Trends

Completed 1994

Corporate Headquarters and Warehouse

In many regions of the country, tilt-up concrete construction is the vernacular of our time. Southern California has seen the construction of acres of tilt-up buildings, usually in the form of warehouses. Curiously, architects have had little positive impact on this effort. Except for Irving Gill and Rudolph Schindler, twentieth-century architects have generally tried to defeat the simple logic and advantages inherent in the system.

Foreston Trends is a 100,000-square-foot warehouse and corporate headquarters for a large distribution company. The site is located in a rather bland office park of similar-sized structures adjacent to a freeway in Southern California. Taking the form of a straightforward and basic box, the project was an attempt to create architecture within the logic of the construction system.

A four-cornered box with punched windows was the point of departure. The economics of the panelized roof system suggested a forty-five-bay plan. The corner bay is devoted to office functions and is elevated to avoid the usual dead space overhead. A low-ceilinged area under the office is now available for ground-level storage and support spaces. There was only one other intervention: the bay adjacent to the offices is an interior entrance court to allow room for a handicapped ramp.

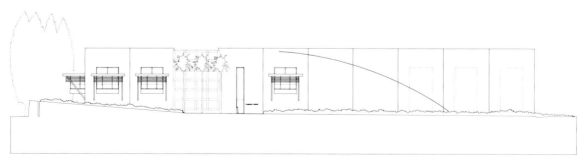

Front elevation

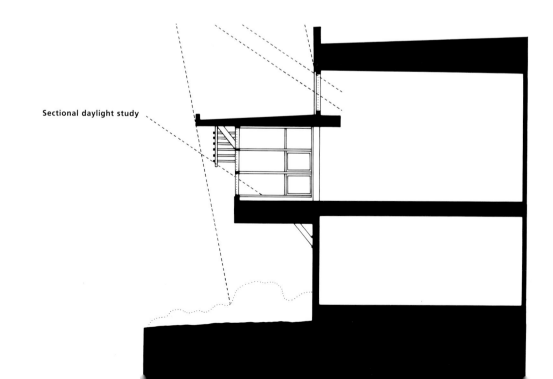

Sectional daylight study

Del Prado

Completed 1992

Part of the redevelopment of a full city block in downtown Los
Angeles, this multilevel, mixed-use structure anchors the
south end of Grand Hope Park. It contains primarily
market-rate apartments, with retail space on the ground
floor and, on the second floor, small neighborhood commercial spaces and a major restaurant. A grand stairway at
a fountain designed by Lawrence Halprin marks the
entrance to the restaurant.

Unique massing divides the project in two parts, each with
its own identity and urban design role. The twenty-story
Tower Building anchors the southeast corner of the park.
Its multilevel facade conveys the energy and enthusiasm of
the nearby Fashion Institute of Design and Merchandising
and the fountain, culminating in a shaded rooftop terrace.

By contrast, the ten-story Arcade Building is a simple and
subdued backdrop to the park's lush plantings. A four-story
pedestrian arcade at the Hope Street promenade accents
the facade. This arcade is intended as a great public room
filled with shops and outdoor restaurants, and marks the
southern entrance to the park. Interior architecture and
apartment layouts are by others.

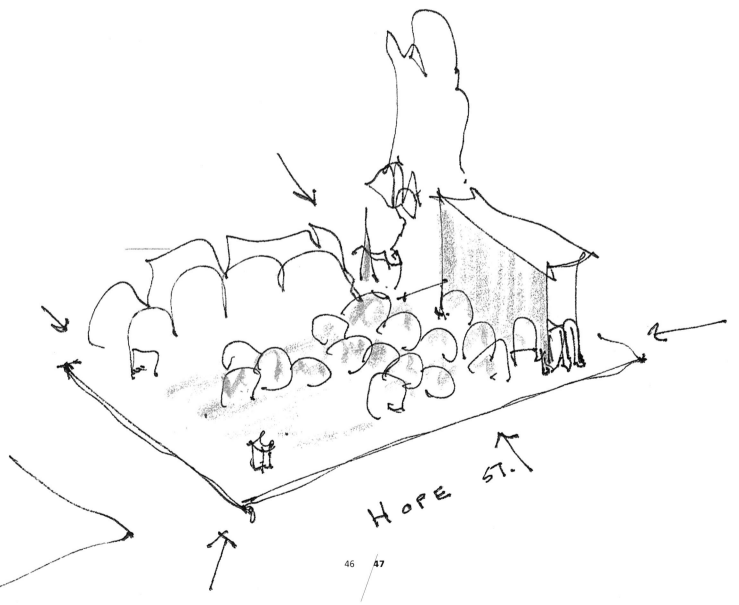

HOPE ST.

Public Buildings

With the demise of both the church and town square as social catalysts in America, the neighborhood community center has become an important civic building type, providing communities with a focus and heart.

Sherman Heights Community Center

Completed 1994

Sherman Heights is an older, crime-plagued but vibrant, multicultural residential neighborhood close to San Diego's core. Other than this center, its only amenity is an elementary school across the street.

The Sherman Heights Community Center was created through a series of bilingual community workshops in which participants actively determined the building program, architectural image, and urban character of the center and an adjacent park. As a result of this process, the community confidently gave the architect artistic control that is generally unafforded by the normally conservative and bureaucratic relationship between architect and city.

The project consists of a new building of about 12,500 square feet, a restored, two-story Victorian house built in 1890, and an adjacent pocketpark that was enlarged and relocated. The new facility contains small meeting and counseling rooms, a large multipurpose space, and a child care center with a kitchen. The historic house was converted to administrative offices, a boardroom, and living space for a full-time caretaker.

The park was dilapidated and often the site of undesirable activity. The new design expands and reconfigures the park as an elaborate, functional forecourt to the new structure. Trellises and vine-covered walls will soon extend the park vertically along the building facades. A "tot-lot" contains much-needed play equipment, and children can be supervised from the community center's front porch. An open-air entry courtyard reinforces neighborhood traditions, creating a seamless transition from park to structure. Traditional elements such as the covered porch and veranda animate this garden court.

The self-contained, ground-level child care center is designed to serve sixty children in four classrooms. It has access to the kitchen and two separate, secure outdoor play areas.

The second-level multipurpose space soars to a height of twenty-five feet, allowing sunlight to filter in from above and reflecting community pride. This flexible space can be divided into as many as six spaces depending on the occasion. It seats two hundred people and accommodates functions such as lectures, performances, banquets, parties, and large community meetings. The space is intimate for a small group meeting and spacious for a capacity crowd.

A fireplace enhances the upper conference room. Views from this room, the upper veranda, and the deck reach to the sea.

As the community requested, this project's image is both domestic and civic, traditional and contemporary—qualities that mirror the rich, diverse values of Sherman Heights.

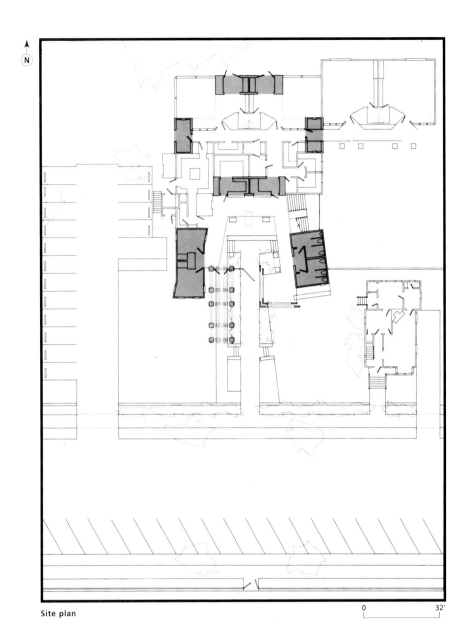

Site plan

0   32'

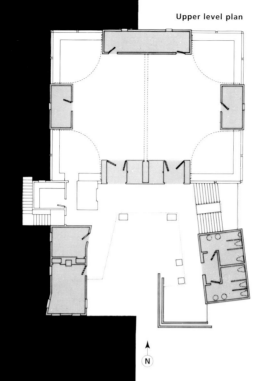

Upper level plan

N

Linda Vista Library

Completed 1987

The Linda Vista Library, a 10,000-square-foot branch facility in a San Diego suburb, serves as a community focal point and cultural center. This civic anchor is located at the corner of a major intersection, adjacent to a shopping center. Tall cypress trees planted at the edges of the intersection delineate a public forecourt where a diagonal entry sequence begins, culminating at a rotunda. A second entry sequence begins in the shopping center parking lot and follows the same diagonal path.

The rotunda projects the desired civic image, accommodates the necessary double entrance, and establishes a simple biaxial geometry that allows the two-person staff to monitor the space. Courtyards expand the rooms and take advantage of the mild climate.

The project is a contemporary translation of regional design and cultural issues, historically represented by delicate vines and wrought iron played against massive adobe walls. Natural, "masculine" materials such as raw steel and concrete block play against "feminine" counterpoints such as torchère lamps and the wood structure. The (apparent) weight of the exterior massing and the buoyant, interior celebration of lightweight stick framing honestly address regional, Hispanic stylistic traditions and the reality of economical wood-frame construction. The exposed joists on the ceiling are covered with perforated metal to absorb sound. Sandblasted concrete block anchors the rotunda and acts as a passive heat sink.

Natural light illuminates the interior. Librarians can select one of four simple switches to control the light level, depending on four lighting conditions: sunny daytime, cloudy daytime, nighttime, unoccupied nighttime. Typical daytime illumination requires only table-mounted task lamps.

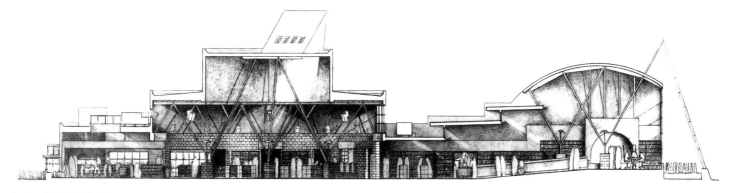

Sectional Daylight Study

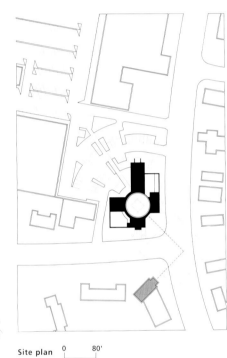

Site plan 0 ____ 80'

N

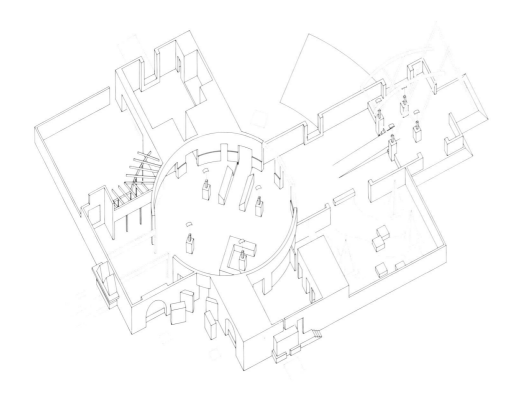

Escondido Transit Center

Completed 1990

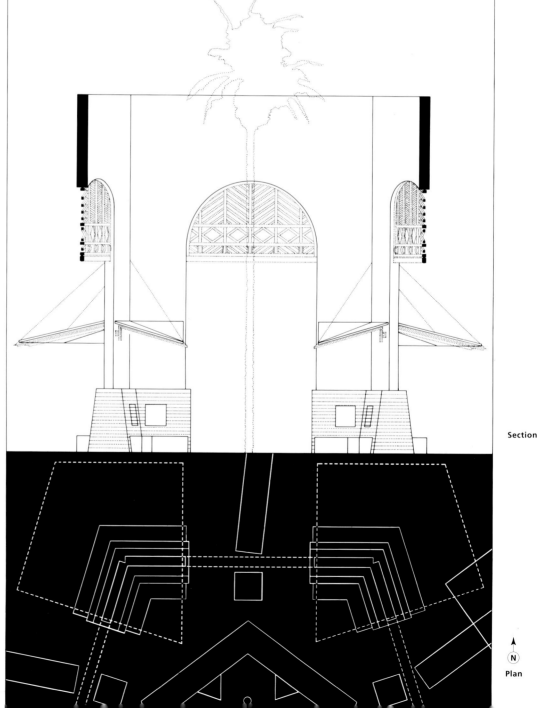

Section

Plan

The Escondido Transit Center was conceived as the masculine partner to the the stucco-clad Escondido City Hall, with its gracious, delicate charm. The city hall complex gives Escondido's urban visual anarchy a regional stylistic direction. This Transit Center, about a mile away, is Escondido's second new civic building. As a front door to the city hall, the Transit Center must relate to and introduce the civic center without competing with it.

The Transit Center's distinct civic role and functional program are celebrated with straightforward materials and simple slab forms, accented with details or quotations (decorative grillwork arches, clock-tower shapes) taken quite literally from the civic center. This reference by "collage" avoids nostalgia and allows for the use of technical imagery appropriate to a modern transportation center.

The pentagonal Great Hall, filled with palm trees and people, is the center's reception room and fountainhead. Shaded pedestrian colonnades radiate from the Great Hall and reach deep into the parking lots. Large clock towers orient the expansive lots, which are carefully choreographed around a historic grove of eucalyptus trees. These towers also serve as gateways at the points of the worst pedestrian/vehicle traffic.

The Transit Center uses only three sizes of concrete panels and low-cost, tilt-up construction techniques.

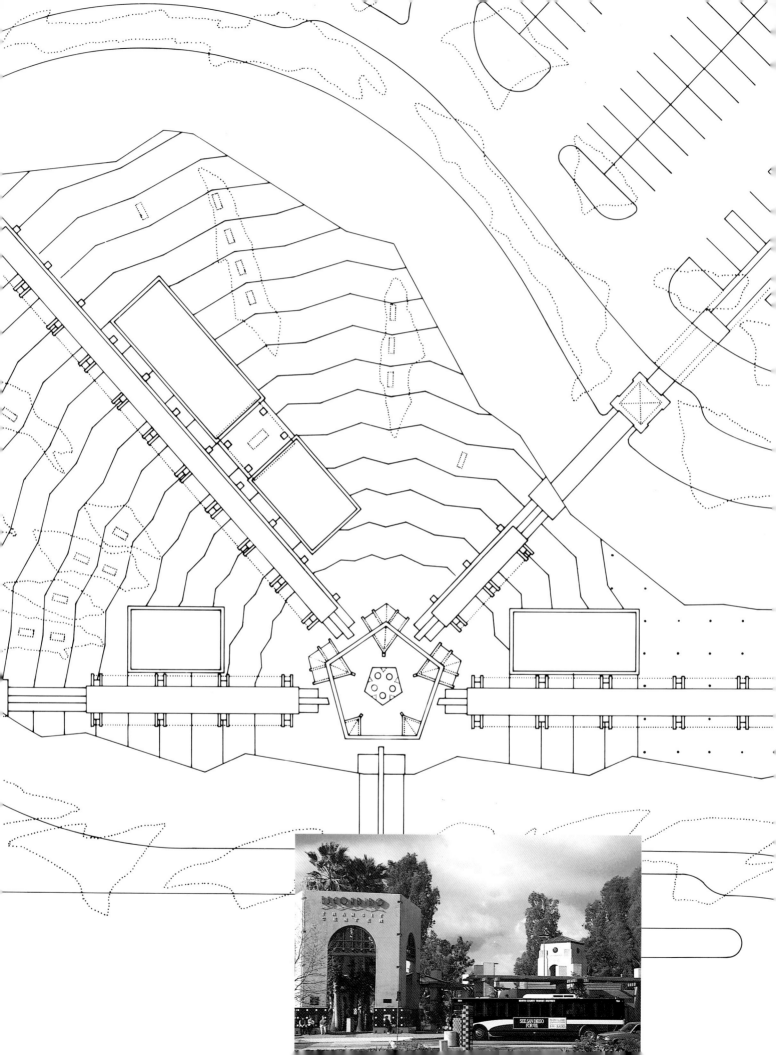

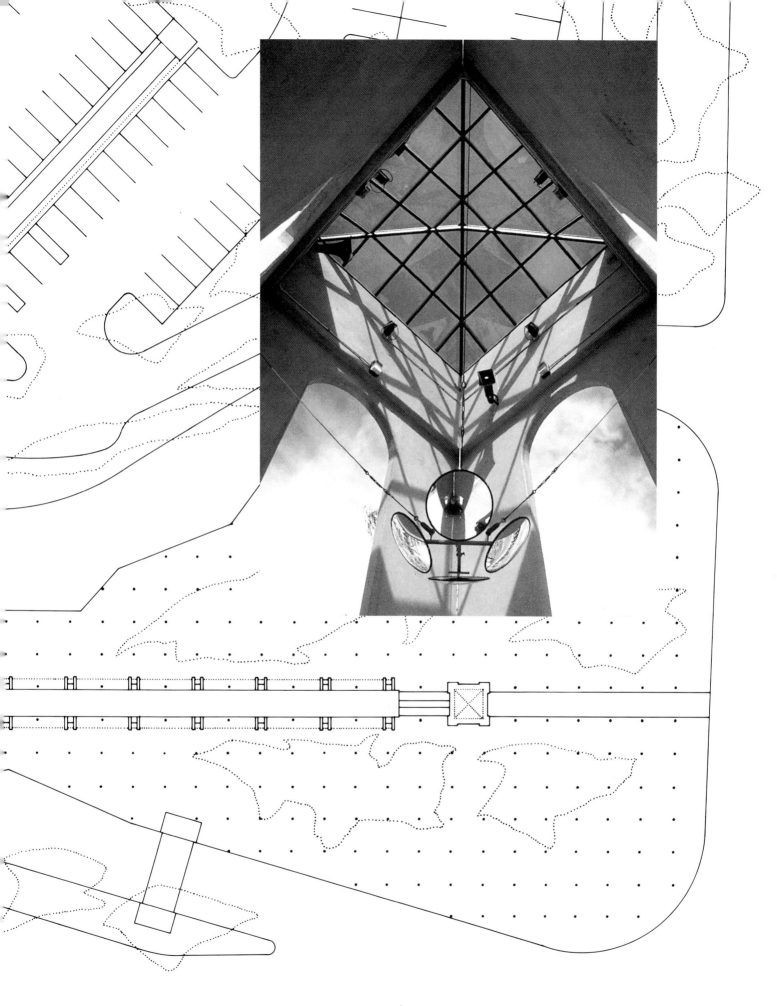

Tustin Ranch Clubhouse and Community Center

Completed 1990

The Tustin Ranch Clubhouse and Community Center is intended to be not only a center for a golf club but also a social focus for the surrounding community, a new neighborhood of several thousand Mediterranean- or Spanish-style houses by other architects.

A modest circular courtyard defines the geographic and social center for both golf course and community. In the tradition of arid climate architecture, the stark forms of the entrance facade reveal softer, more richly detailed layers as one proceeds through the building. Cascading dining terraces form the final element in this sequence as the structure transitions to the green fairways.

The difficult building program required a 300-seat dining space that could be subdivided into smaller spaces. This concept was inverted by creating an intimate and defined dining room, bar/lounge, and pro shop/foyer that can function as a single large space. Folding translucent panels and tall trophy cases on wheels allow for various degrees of enclosure.

The structure does not mimic the surrounding housing forms but does rely on the materials and colors of the neighborhood to maintain continuity and compatibility. Although modern in detail and execution, heavy stucco walls and shaded arcades are more reminiscent of the dignity and romance of early adobe missions than of thin-walled residential construction.

As in early California Hispanic architecture, simple plaster surfaces contrast with the richness of layered wood ceilings, the fragility of delicate metal detail, and the lacelike tracery of flowering vines to achieve an intimate scale.

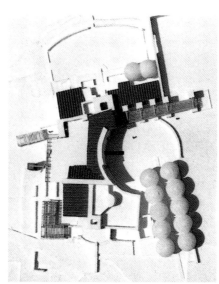

The video viewing room at the La Jolla Museum of Contemporary Art is a site-specific work designed and realized in response to the museum's environment. The museum's exhibition/installation series aims to integrate newly developed, experimental art forms into the museum context.

The museum requested an inviting but neutral space for viewing video. The architect responded by using a twelve-foot-square janitorial storage room conceived as a "video porch." This concept gave the small storage room a unique identity and established a logical relationship to the adjacent gallery.

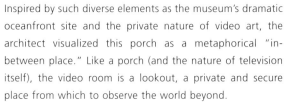

Video Porch,
La Jolla Museum of
Contemporary Art

Completed 1984

Inspired by such diverse elements as the museum's dramatic oceanfront site and the private nature of video art, the architect visualized this porch as a metaphorical "in-between place." Like a porch (and the nature of television itself), the video room is a lookout, a private and secure place from which to observe the world beyond.

The room is adjacent to the seaward wall of the original Scripps House (1915) designed by Irving Gill, which is now encased within the museum structure. The architect acknowledged the video room's relationship to the original house by carefully peeling back the various layers of remodeling, as in an archaeological dig, to reveal Gill's original concrete wall.

Rich in color and texture, and in striking contrast to the main gallery, this layered wall marks the entrance to the video room, screened from view by an oblique partition. A miniature television monitor at the end of the screen wall registers an image of the room's interior. Behind the protective wall, past the newly revealed Gill wall, lies the porch. Passing through layers of the building's history to reach a portion of the original residential structure sets a domestic tone appropriate to the act of watching television or video, and introduces the visitor to the room's boldly delineated form and essentially informal nature.

Inside the room, a semitransparent scrim stretched between pipe supports creates an illusion of depth and space. Warm lighting adds subtle intrigue to the soft shapes of the exposed construction beyond the scrim. The intent was to avoid upstaging the video artists while providing a provocative environment.

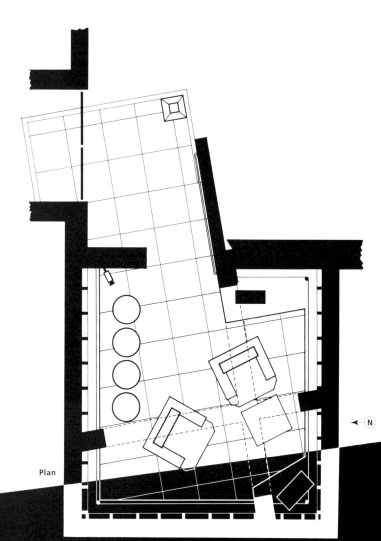

Plan

Early Childhood Education Center

Completed 1995

This project adds three new classrooms to the Early Childhood Education Center at the University of California at San Diego. The existing facility consists of two well-detailed, high-tech-style, one-story structures.

Rather than extend or compete with the buoyant existing architecture, this minimalist addition provides a background and visual anchor. In fact, the addition eventually will seem to have been built before the existing structures.

Materials derive from the existing buildings: four-inch concrete block and white painted metal. A four-foot-thick masonry wall grounds the entire complex and is "inhabited" by cozy window seats, coat closets, storage areas, and hideouts. Controlled clerestory light animates the classrooms, and low, child-scale roofs provide a protected transition to the play areas outside.

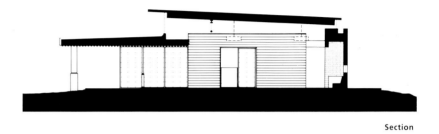

Section

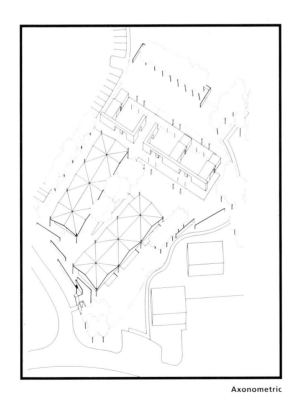

Axonometric

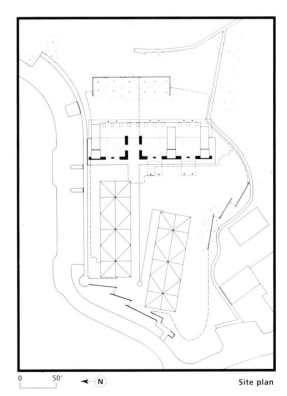

0   50'   ◄ N   Site plan

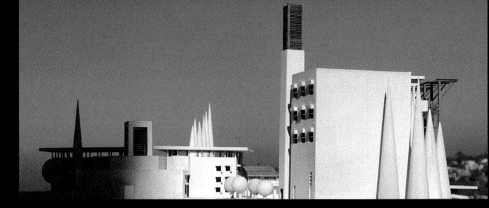

The design of a school of architecture holds a special fascination for all architects. For the community and the entire state, such a facility can become a regional focus for architecture.

the core of the design challenge is a fascinating paradox: The building must be a strong statement with an identifiable image yet be stylistically neutral—like an artist's loft.

More than with any other facility on campus, it must be possible for both faculty and students to "own" this building and make it theirs. Like the purposeful neutrality of a well-planned theater stage, this building must admit and nurture unforeseen and unforeseeable personalities, attitudes, and events.

Furthermore, the architecture must spawn a delicate and often conflicting set of social concerns essential to the pursuit of original and significant creative work. It must encourage student/student and student/faculty interaction (both spontaneous and calculated) while allowing, and even promoting, the solitude and introspection so necessary to this work.

Interestingly, both traditional, academic architecture and signature architecture are inappropriate and even irrelevant models for this project. This must not be a signature building, but rather a building ready for signatures. To that end, its perimeter curved wall at the entrance to the campus provides a place for all graduates' names to be sandblasted into the concrete in recognition of their academic achievement.

New architecture facilities rarely explore the educational opportunities inherent in the design and construction of the facility itself. In this scheme the buildings themselves serve as laboratories for student exploration, analysis, and observation. The students are intentionally placed in sensitive, but not uncomfortable, contact with the desert environment.

In addition, the buildings serve as textbooks for design and construction concepts. For instance, each of the major building construction and environmental support systems is exposed for the purpose of teaching architectural design and building technology courses.

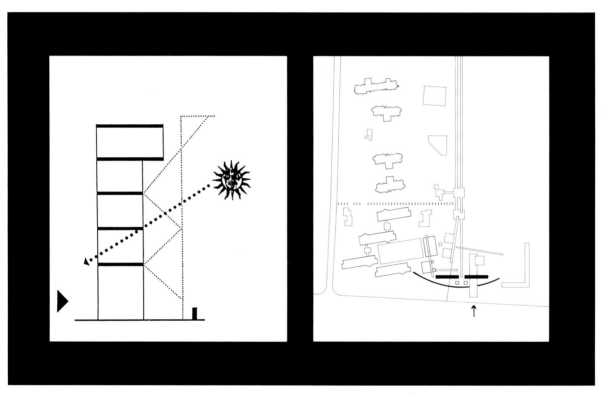

Solar orientation   University gateway

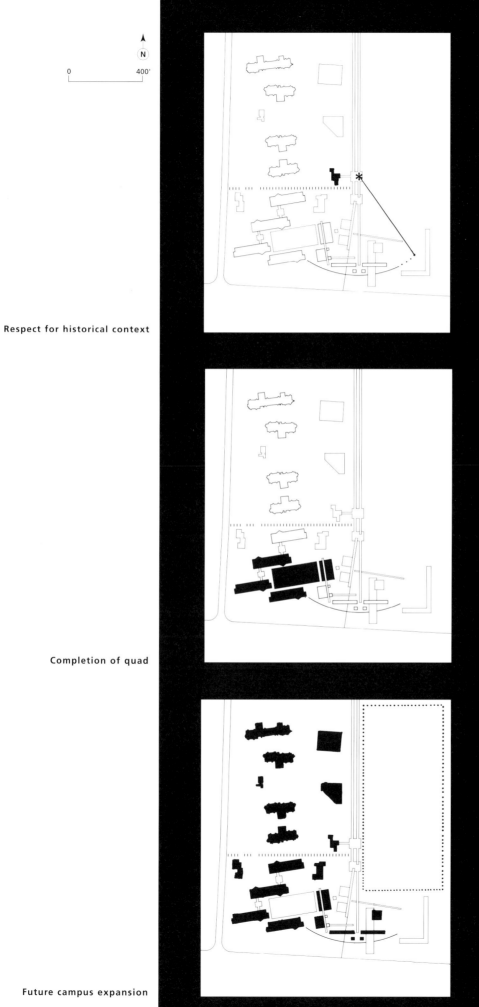

0 400' N

Respect for historical context

Completion of quad

Future campus expansion

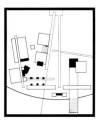

Porches

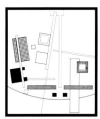

Textbook building

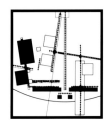

Theater

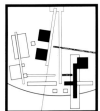

Public buildings

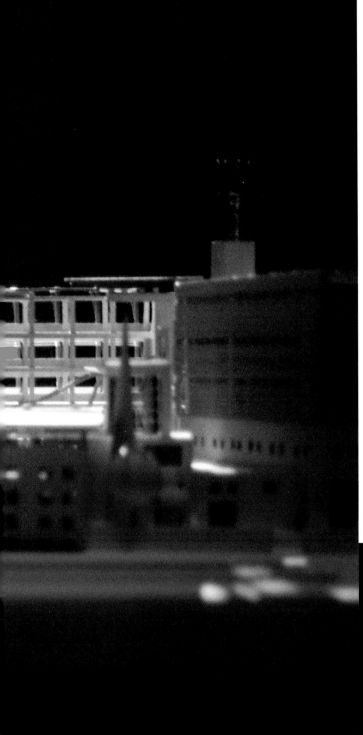

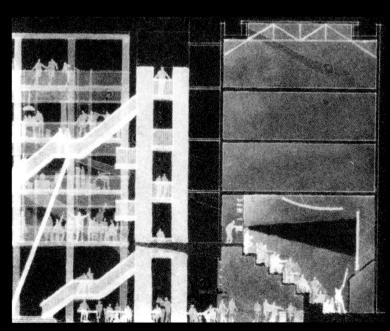

Section

Student court

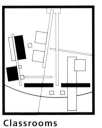

Classrooms

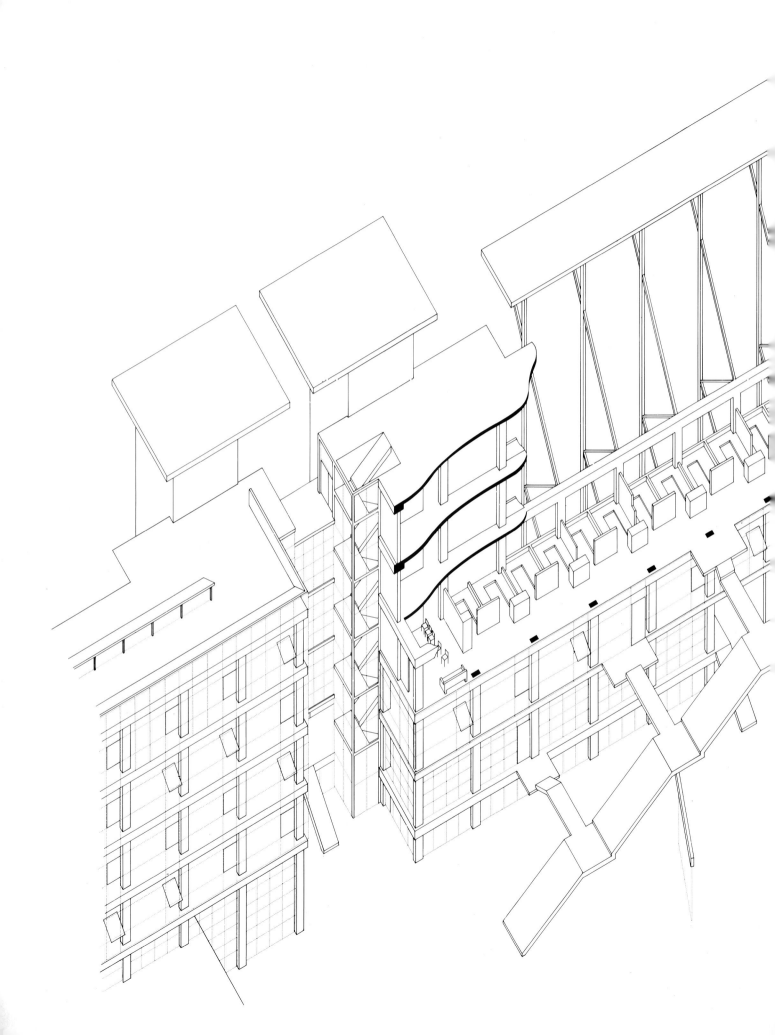

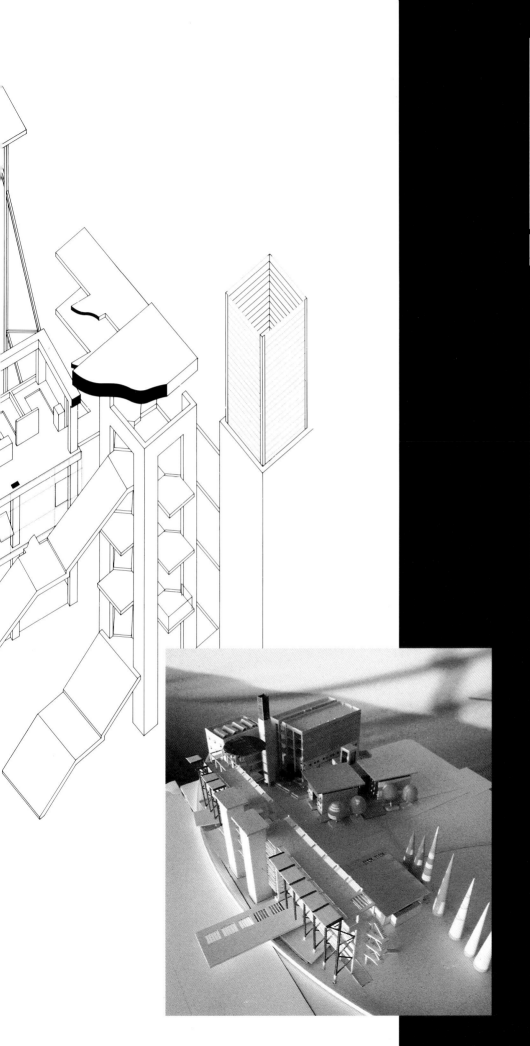

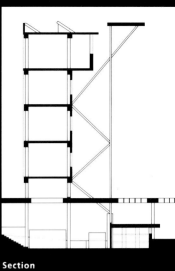

Section

North elevation of studios

Balboa Park Activity Center

Commissioned 1994

The Balboa Park Activity Center will be the first large construction in Balboa Park since the 1950s. The 35,500-square-foot, one-story structure will house facilities for volleyball, badminton, table tennis, and special events. Tilt-up concrete walls contain the large, flexible space.

The approach to the center is from an existing parking lot, up a wide formal stair to a walled courtyard, both in the Balboa Park tradition. To the south, a rustic garden is a soft forecourt to the main building entry and offers places to sit and enjoy the sweeping views of downtown San Diego.

The simple, light-filled entry five feet above the gym floor provides a single control point and overlooks the activities below. Ramped walkways lead from the entry under an arcade of concrete buttresses to the midpoint of the activities floor. A balcony on the north side is accessible from a large turfed green.

Unlike a basketball gym, here all sources of direct light or glare must be eliminated. The concrete walls tilt outward to let soft overhead light enter discreetly. Other skylights and windows are carefully baffled and screened. For special events, direct sunlight may be admitted by raising large, roll-up shutters.

Although contemporary in design and detail, the Activity Center joins the family of Balboa Park buildings built for world expositions in 1915 and 1935. Both the building's proportions and planning concepts follow Beaux-Arts tradition. The center is carefully sighted on a knoll overlooking the city and will become the southern terminus of an existing formal axis of fountains and gardens.

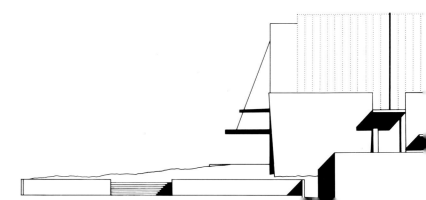

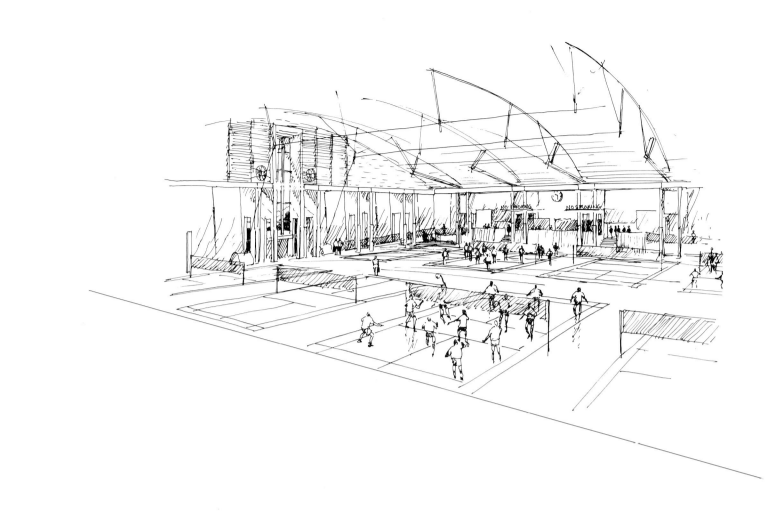

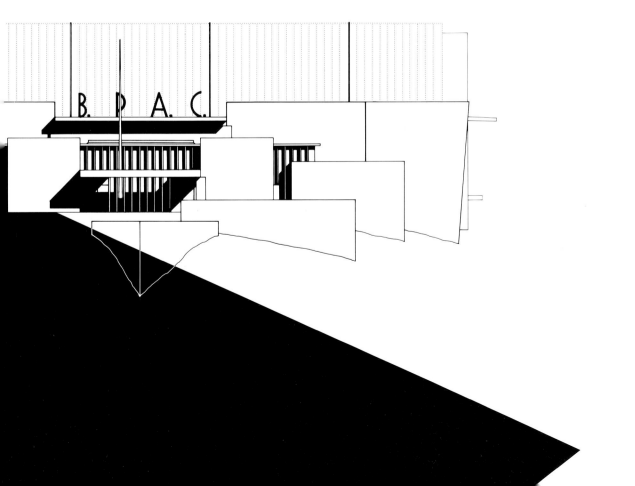

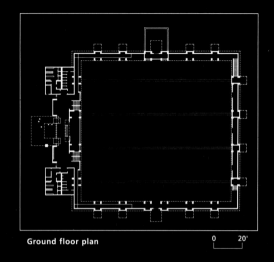

Ground floor plan

0   20'

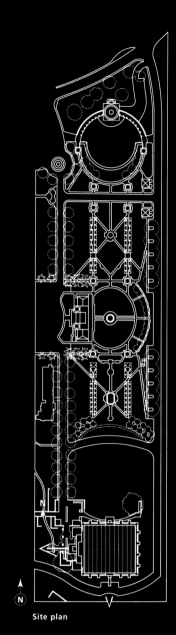

N

Site plan

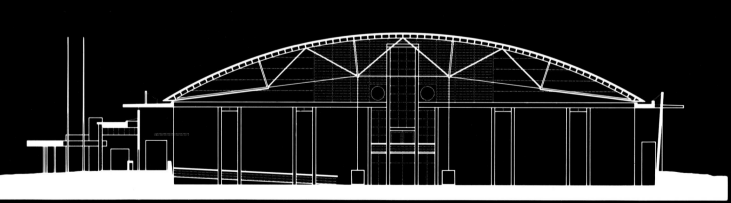

Section

St. David's Episcopal Church

Commissioned 1992

St. David's Episcopal Church was partially destroyed by arson in 1991. A new master plan retains the still-standing Parish Hall and transforms it into an educational wing. This building, with its modest arcade, becomes one side of a cloistered court surrounded by a new 300-seat church, parish hall, and administration wing with library. The three-acre site in an older, residential neighborhood in San Diego fronts a broadly curved, busy street and slopes down in back to a preschool play yard and undeveloped canyon. A 30-seat chapel next to the original parish hall faces the canyon; in contrast, the church is oriented inward.

The complex addresses several fascinating paradoxes that crystallized in workshop sessions with the congregation, who requested that the project be:

- inviting, welcoming, and open to the neighborhood,
  but at the same time private and secluded;
- a joyous place of vibrant social interaction, but a quiet
  place for private introspection and peaceful prayer;
- familiar, common, and unpretentious,
  but special and unique;
- straightforward, practical, and functional,
  but spiritually transcendent;
- built with exquisite detail and handcrafted care,
  but inexpensive.

The square plan of the church determines the proportions of the cloister and orders both the chapel and the parking lot. The parking lot, programmatically the largest area, is a series of overlapping squares of asphalt, citrus trees, and compacted earth.

The site is organized by an axis that begins at the altar, links the baptismal font/steeple and chapel court, and ends at a discreet fountain. Centered on the glass steeple is a formal gated entry from busy Milton Street. A third, more secluded entry is through a eucalyptus grove.

The church was conceived as a "House of the People of God" rather than a "House of God." The square plan and floor-level chancel emphasize community and togetherness, yet avoid a functional but very secular amphitheater layout. Removable kneelers and altar offer flexibility.

The darkened narthex is entered from one of three doors. Light enters only through the skylight/steeple above a stone baptismal font. The low, eight-foot concrete ceiling reflects sound down to the dry-laid, slightly undulating brick floor. The brittle acoustics and hard surfaces of the narthex contrast with soft-covered doors that slide open to reveal the main sanctuary. Dappled light floods in overhead from a roof of 2' x 8' wood planks separated by 5/8" clear plastic spines. A hidden skylight reflects eastern sunlight onto a wall behind the simple cross.

A curved, two-foot-high concrete wall in the sanctuary was inspired by Gunnar Asplund's Woodland Chapel (1918–20) in Stockholm. It creates a more intimate inner seating area, solves the problem of the sloping floor, and allows for ritual candle lighting. The wall is a layered, soft counterpoint to the primary shape of the square plan.

A church must seem intimate and well-attended even if a particular ceremony involves only a small gathering. To achieve this, only 160 seats were built as fixed pews. Movable chairs increase seating to 227 in the inner area, while adding folding chairs in the flat area on the perimeter accommodates 340 people, with further expansion available on the south patio and in the narthex for Easter and Christmas services.

Like the church, the proportions of the new parish hall are based on squares and the principle of the Golden Section. The hall is served from a single kitchen even when divided into three separate meeting rooms. A brick-paved, walled courtyard shaded by a single California sycamore provides a coffee area and expansion space for both the parish hall and the church.

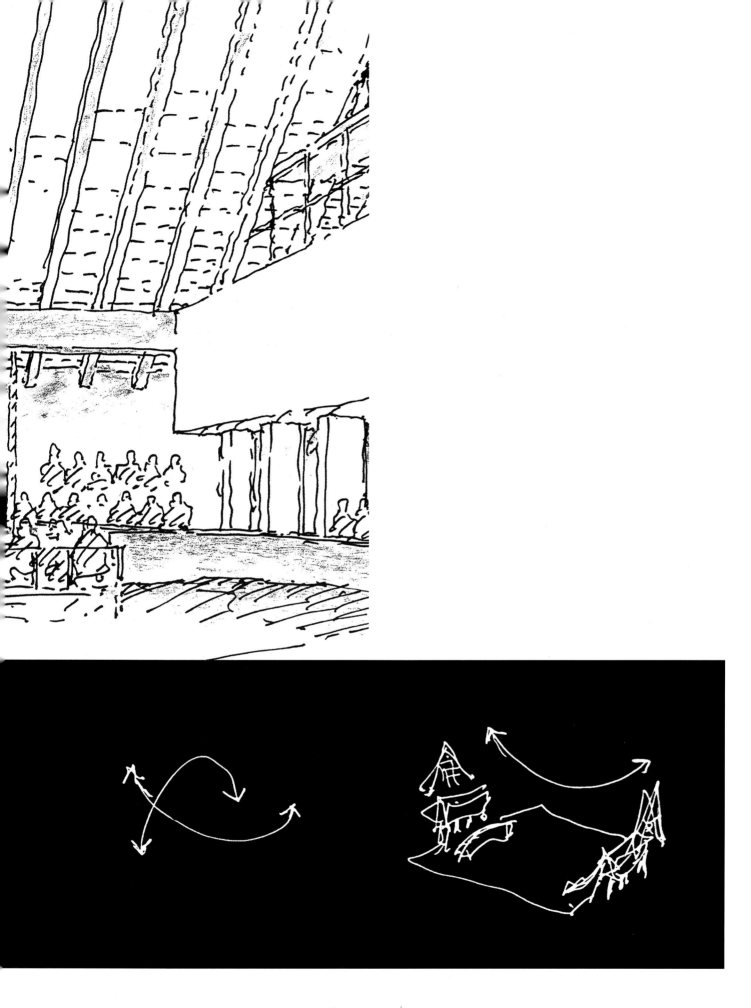

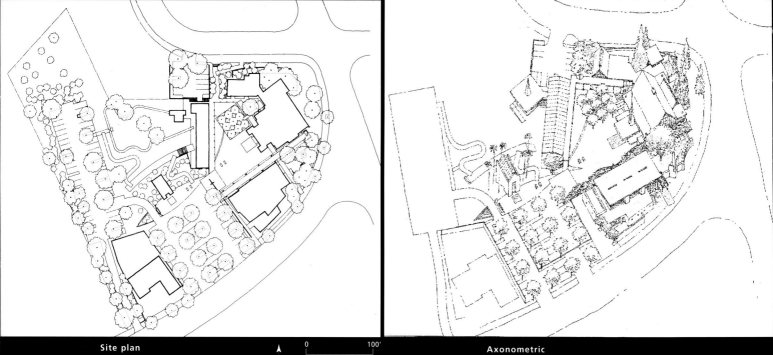

Site plan   0   100'

Axonometric

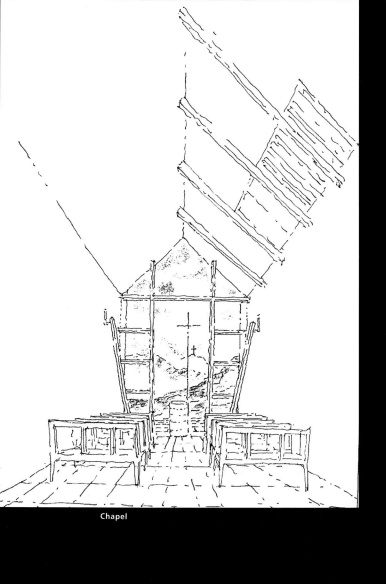

Chapel

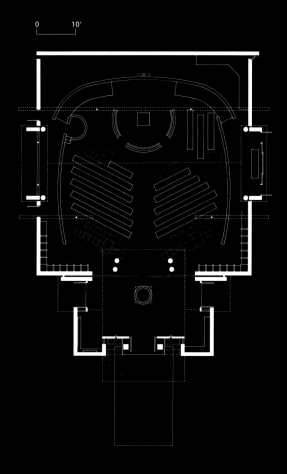

Floor plan

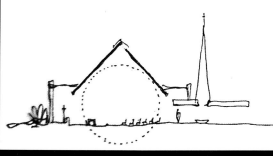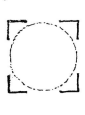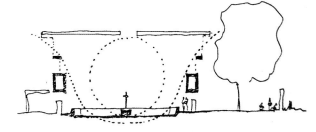

Section concept

Affordable Housing

The single room occupancy (SRO) hotel houses primarily low-income and transient residents and is often the last housing option available before homelessness. Over the last several decades, robust development in San Diego has gradually displaced a limited stock of SROs.

202 Island Inn is an HUD-subsidized, low-cost SRO hotel at the edge of downtown San Diego's Chinese district. The four-story building includes 197 units above a 91-space basement parking structure and ground-level retail and live/work spaces. Large, light-filled rooms with private bathrooms and kitchenettes create living spaces not unlike small studio apartments. Amenities include a reading room, recreation room, lounge, laundry, and vending area.

Each of the three different street facades responds to its particular urban design opportunities. The Third Avenue elevation, while contemporary in materials and execution, is carefully scaled to the adjacent historic buildings. Their turn-of-the-century typology—wrought iron balcony, mission tile eyebrow, and shaped parapet—was reinterpreted to create compatibility without cute nostalgia. Live/work spaces at street level have their own entrances.

202 Island Inn

Completed 1992

The main entrance on Island Avenue is a more abstract composition, inspired by adjacent warehouses as well as formal images of classic hotels. The underground garage entry is leveraged to create a generous-sized, landscaped forecourt, a rare amenity for this unusually dense urban building type. An open but protected front porch is an active social focal point and provides the light court's required fire exit. Pedestrians can see through the porch into the landscaped central courtyard. A recreation room and Cafe 222 further animate the corner and the street.

The colorful, dynamic exuberance of the Second Street facade contrasts with the hotel architecture and comments on the dark brown condominium towers anchoring the other end of the street. Large stucco planes unfold and tilt to favor the south sun.

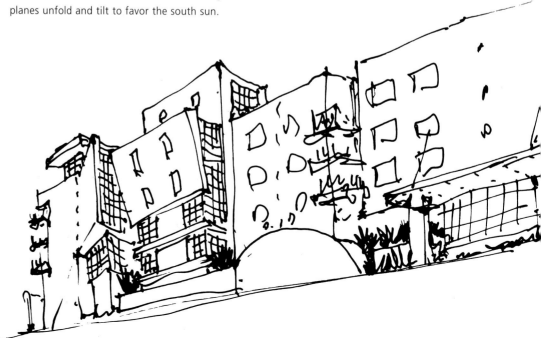

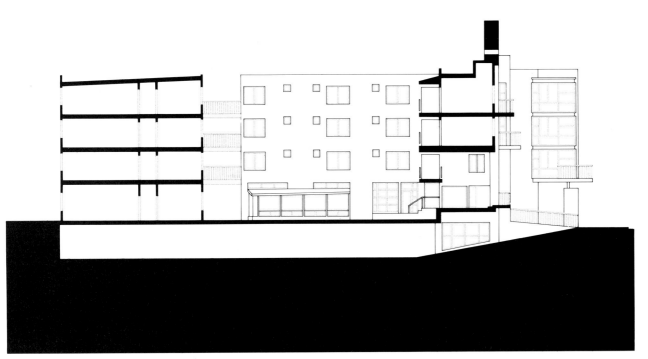

Section A

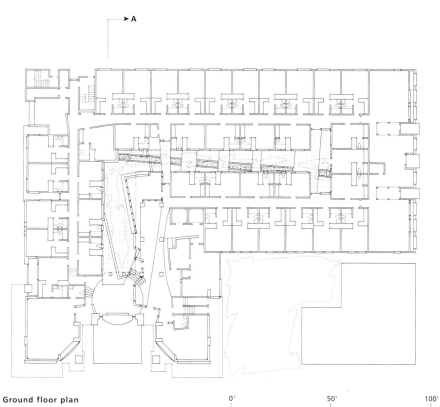

Ground floor plan

0'   50'   100'

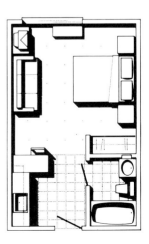

Typical unit plan

Third Street elevation

Esperanza Garden Apartments

Completed 1994

As the first new affordable-housing project built in Encinitas in twenty years, Esperanza Garden Apartments is expected to serve as a model for similar infill projects in other communities. The residents are families that meet certain income requirements dictated by the funding sources.

Designed through a series of participatory workshops with neighbors, this ten-unit project focuses on a central communal play area and gathering spot. It is patterned after the classic bungalow courts throughout Southern California. The units are clustered to promote interaction among the residents, while allowing privacy in individual, fenced backyards.

Each two-story unit features a front porch and kitchen oriented to the central courtyard to allow supervision of children at play. A standardized floor plan contains a kitchen/bathroom plumbing core; a large, flexible living/dining room; and two bedrooms. For construction economy, the three- and four-bedroom plan variations are created simply by adding bedrooms to the basic two-bedroom plan.

After participating in the design workshops, the neighbors, who at first opposed the project, ultimately supported its approval. Construction was provided through a package of private, state, and federal funds.

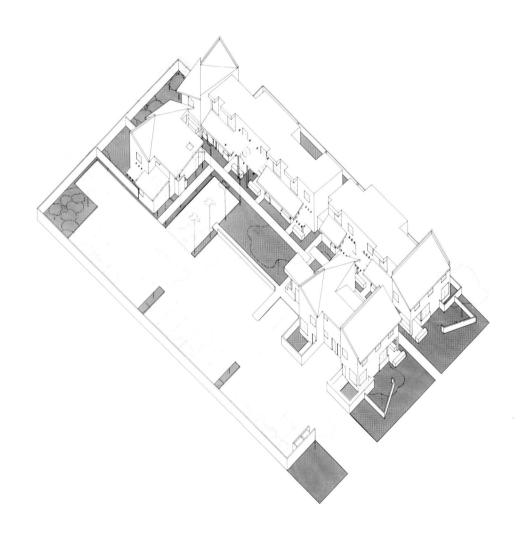

Ground floor plan

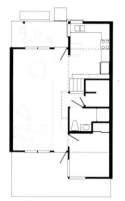

Ground floor plan with bedroom

Two-bedroom upper floor plan

Three-bedroom upper floor plan

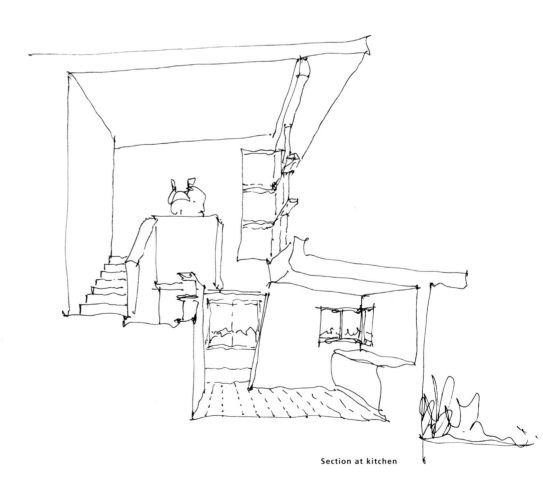

Section at kitchen

La Pensione at India & Date

Completed 1991

This mixed-use project consists of a four-story, 80-room SRO hotel above two street-level restaurants. Underground parking is accessible from Date Street.

The 8,500-square-foot site on India Street is at the heart of what remains of San Diego's historic Italian neighborhood. As the first significant new structure in Little Italy in many years, this SRO's responsibility goes beyond just housing the poor. The project is seen as a model for higher-density development in this one- and two-story neighborhood. Its F.A.R. (Floor/Area Ratio) of four, while significantly smaller than the six allowable, was still potentially overwhelming to the buildings around it.

A historic but structurally inadequate two-story, wood-frame structure formerly occupied the corner of the site. Its facade was retained to anchor the corner and perpetuate the intimate scale of the 50-foot lots in the area. A setback on India Street at the second story respects the street scale. Both restaurants have clear-glass, operable windows and sidewalk tables. A public passageway between the two leads to a light court and patio for outdoor dining, in the tradition of other Little Italy restaurants.

The hotel entrance has its own identity on Date Street. Although the rooms are small and efficient, they have nine-foot ceilings and are filled with light.

B ← → A

N

Ground floor plan

Typical upper level plan

Section A

Section B

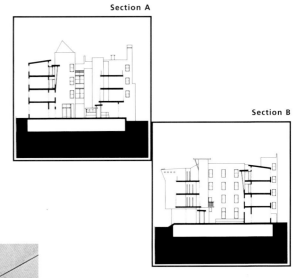

The J Street Inn offers affordable housing for San Diego's working poor. This low-cost, for-profit project by a private developer was completed with close cooperation and assistance from the Centre City Development Corporation and the city planning department.

The Inn is four stories of wood-frame construction over a concrete parking garage and contains a lobby, library, laundry, and exercise room. Each of the 221 rooms has a private bath and a kitchen with a microwave, making the Inn the first built example of the city's new living unit ordinance.

A central light court, narrow due to the density requirements of the project, was treated as a site-specific sculpture. It contains a grove of fast-growing bamboo and a waterfall that masks noise from the rooms.

Low cost was achieved by using standard housing detailing and simple, boxlike forms. Two architectural events animate these forms, one on Second Avenue at the library, and a second, more enthusiastic celebration at the corner entry. A public deck on each floor permits secure but visible activity. Since the Inn's opening, the upper deck has been used almost constantly. To further enliven the street, all common rooms are located along Second Avenue.

Two high-rise towers of luxury condominiums were subsequently built across the street, fulfilling San Diego's goal of mixed-use vitality.

J Street Inn

Completed 1990

The Baltic Inn contains 204 rooms, 10' x 12' and 10' x 16'. Each room features an innovative, standardized built-in wall unit with toilet, sink, storage space, closet, refrigerator, and TV. Common showers are on every floor. Common areas on the ground floor include the lobby, TV lounge, vending area, bicycle storage, and laundry. Interior light courts allow natural light and ventilation in the corridors and rooms. A small front porch at street level and a second porch above the arched entry encourage the "inhabited" street presence so often missing from minimal urban structures. A tower topped by a neon sculpture gives the building a special identity and carries on San Diego's tower tradition.

The design and construction of the Baltic Inn were funded by a low-interest $500,000 loan from the San Diego Housing Commission and a $2.7 million loan from a private bank. The hotel is a for-profit venture by a private developer.

Like many SROs, the Baltic Inn falls into the regulatory void between a hotel and an apartment building. The developer and the architect negotiated extensively with the building department for approval of creative zoning and building code variances. Following the pioneering development of the Baltic Inn, more than two thousand SRO hotel rooms are now under design or construction in San Diego.

Baltic Inn

Completed 1987

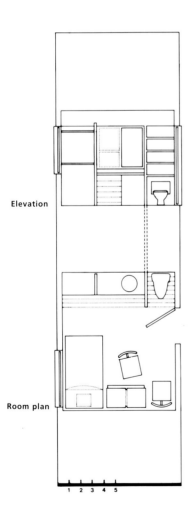

Elevation

Room plan

1 2 3 4 5

Private Houses

Capistrano Beach Glass House

Completed 1993

Capistrano Beach is a small California beachfront community. A single strip of narrow lots is a fragile mediator between the eroding shore to the west and high, windswept bluffs to the east.

The excitement of inhabiting the ocean's edge is translated into a series of architectural juxtapositions: thick walls of poured concrete against glass pavilions; deep shade and dappled light against the sand's harsh glare; exposed, stagelike decks and platforms against veiled privacy.

The 3,700-square-foot house acknowledges its context through its diagram and construction materials. East/west-oriented architectural planes reinforce the rigid, parallel property lines. North/south elements respond more freely to the primal forces at work on the seashore, assuming soft curves and eroded shapes.

To minimize foundation caissons, the structure consists of a two-story, poured-in-place concrete spine with cantilevered concrete floor slabs. The slabs support the wood-frame second-story bedroom walls, which are clad in black asphalt shingles. A series of redwood lattice structures contrasts with the large expanses of glass and the mid-level sundeck and provides shade and privacy.

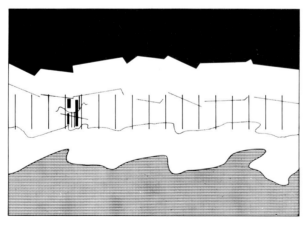

Site plan

N   0   50'

The narrow lot encourages a particular choreography. Through two iron gates on the east side of the property, one enters an intimate, formal vegetable garden surrounded by glass walls six feet high. A concrete "pier" hovering over the sand leads to the front entry porch. This porch faces away from the beach and toward the courtyard garden, which is landscaped as a "suburban artifact."

One enters the house along the sweeping glass garden wall. The sea reveals itself partially at first, then with a sudden completeness at the living room. A row of trees growing along the exterior of the thick fireplace wall will lend shade and privacy to this space. A low-ceilinged dining room contrasts with the tall glass walls of the living pavilion.

A curved stair connects the garden to the sea and leads to the mid-level sundeck. A private bridge at the top of this stair follows the concrete spine to the master suite, which opens to the living room and garden court but is veiled from the sea. The suite contains a library, study, and breakfast table. The spine continues through the master bath and terminates at a circular shower space oriented to the east, for morning light. Two guest suites are above the garage.

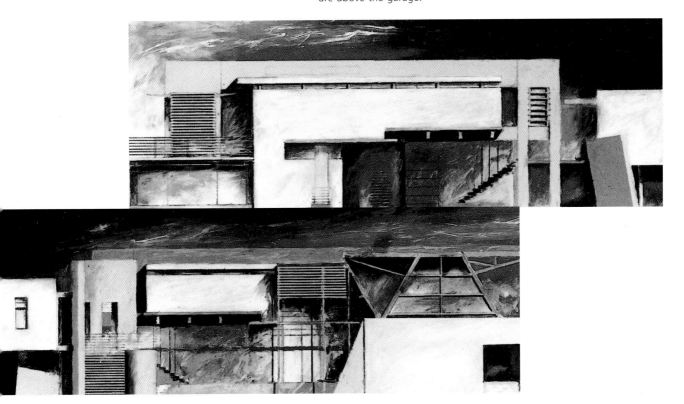

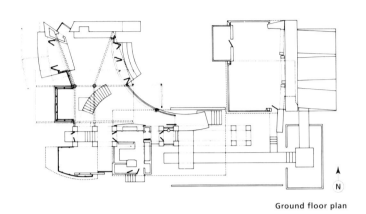

Ground floor plan

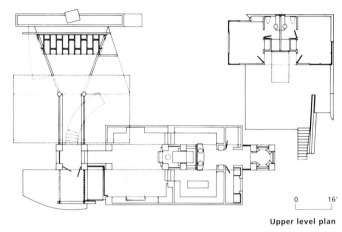

Upper level plan

0   16'

SECTION LOOKING WEST.

Oxley House

Completed 1983

The American dream remains the detached single-family home. This little house explores that dream in the context of today's economic reality.

The Oxley House is a one-room residence for a single woman, with utility rooms and guest quarters at ground level. To the south, an outdoor lath house with movable shades expands the living space, filters the summer sun, and permits direct-gain passive solar heating in winter. The house contains only 700 square feet on each level. The complete cost for the project, including detached garage, was $97,000.

Second level plan

First level plan

N

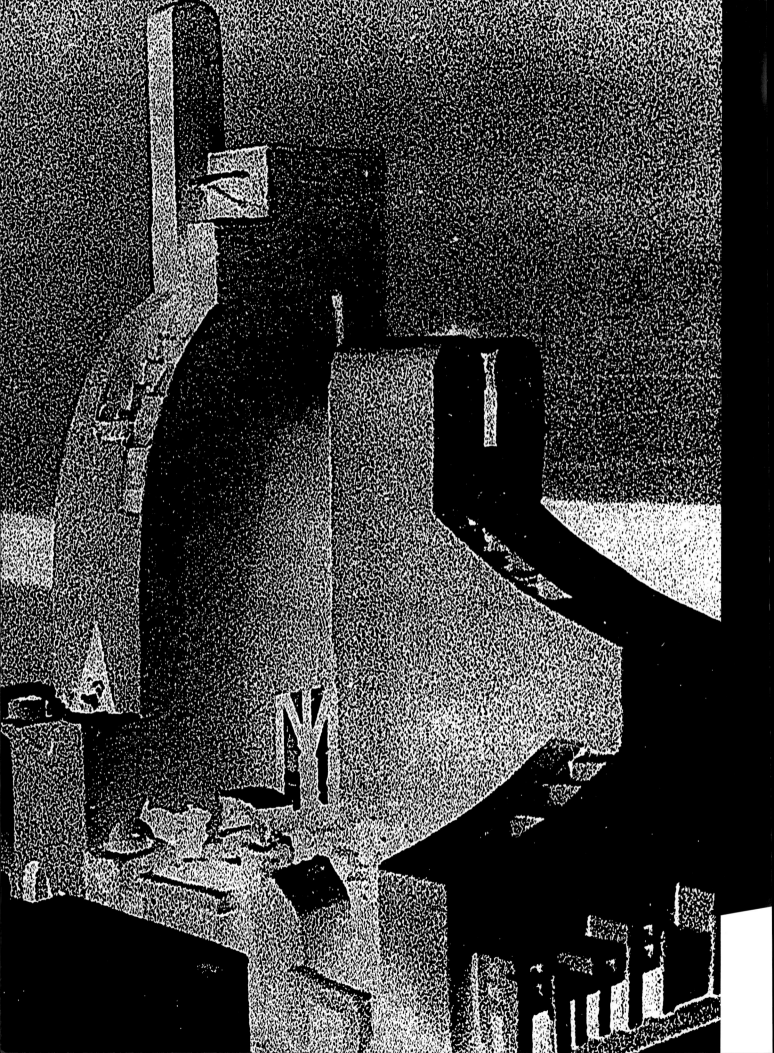

unbuilt
San Diego

By Ann Jarmusch

Downtown San Diego seems perpetually on the cusp of growing into a shimmering cosmopolitan city—a gloriously sited, sun-kissed, urban resort-by-the-sea. Although major downtown redevelopment projects and an attractive historic district now throbbing with nightlife have made progress over the past decade, the goal that San Diego be known for more than beaches, golf courses, and a zoo has thus far eluded its big-city proponents.

Rob Wellington Quigley, who has practiced architecture here for twenty-five years, has contributed a number of daringly designed projects that keep nudging reluctant San Diego onto a richer, livelier path. Given the city's conservative nature, it is surprising that Quigley has risen to the top of his field here and managed to build innovative, experimental, and sometimes playful low-income housing, beach houses, churches, and a nature center.

The constellation of Quigley buildings energizing downtown includes internationally acclaimed single room occupancy hotels (SROs) for the working poor, a hard-won neighborhood community center, and the controversial Beaumont Building, where the architect lives with his family on the top floor and leads his firm on the floor below. With jutting profiles and unusual geometries, these exuberant low-rise structures assert themselves yet nestle into old, established city blocks. All exhibit traces of the upstart and the traditional, surprise and good humor, permanence and magic.

Five unbuilt projects designed for downtown San Diego waterfront or redevelopment sites demonstrate Quigley's design strength, border-style verve, and humanism on large and small scales.

One of the most unorthodox high-rise complexes ever to be designed for San Diego was La Entrada, a competition entry for a large downtown parcel controlled by Centre City Development Corporation, the city's redevelopment arm. The mostly residential but mixed-use project would join large housing complexes on two sides and upscale retail centers to the north.

La Entrada

Designed 1987

Here Quigley boldly experimented on a large scale with some of the regional design "truths" that he engagingly applies to smaller projects and private residences. Among these border-specific elements, he took into account sunlight, waterfront views, indoor-outdoor living spaces, and flower-filled courtyards.

More challenging in a full-block, thirty-six-story, mixed-use complex is contrasting the earth-bound massing of domestic buildings (perhaps concrete or stucco over wood frame) with delicate filtered sunlight or vines across walls or wood pergolas. Irving Gill, San Diego's first modernist architect and one whose work Quigley has studied, explored this delicate balance for years, but always on a small residential scale.

In an unusual move, Quigley sited La Entrada so it would not block sunlight and views of a condominium tower nearby or any future high-rise building to the east. He also oriented the project so most residents would enjoy bay views and catch breezes across a contoured courtyard.

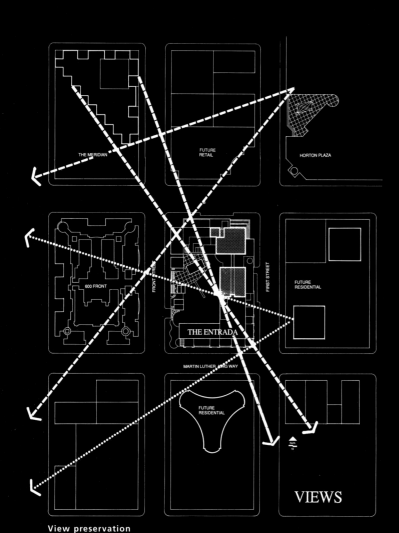

View preservation

View from north

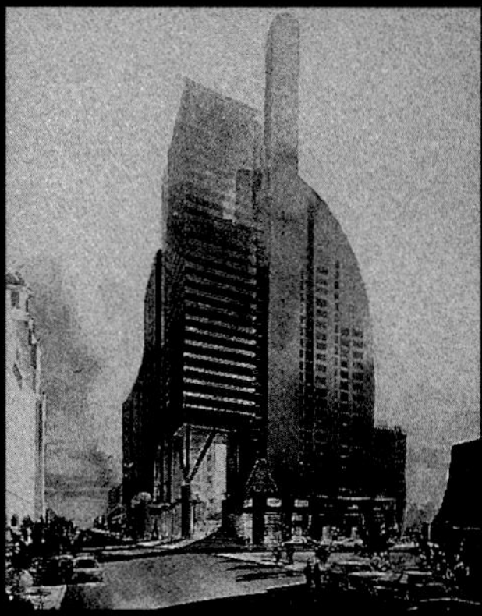

City setting

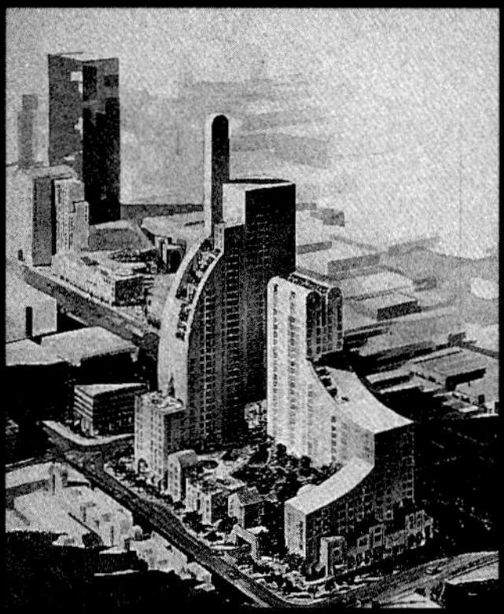

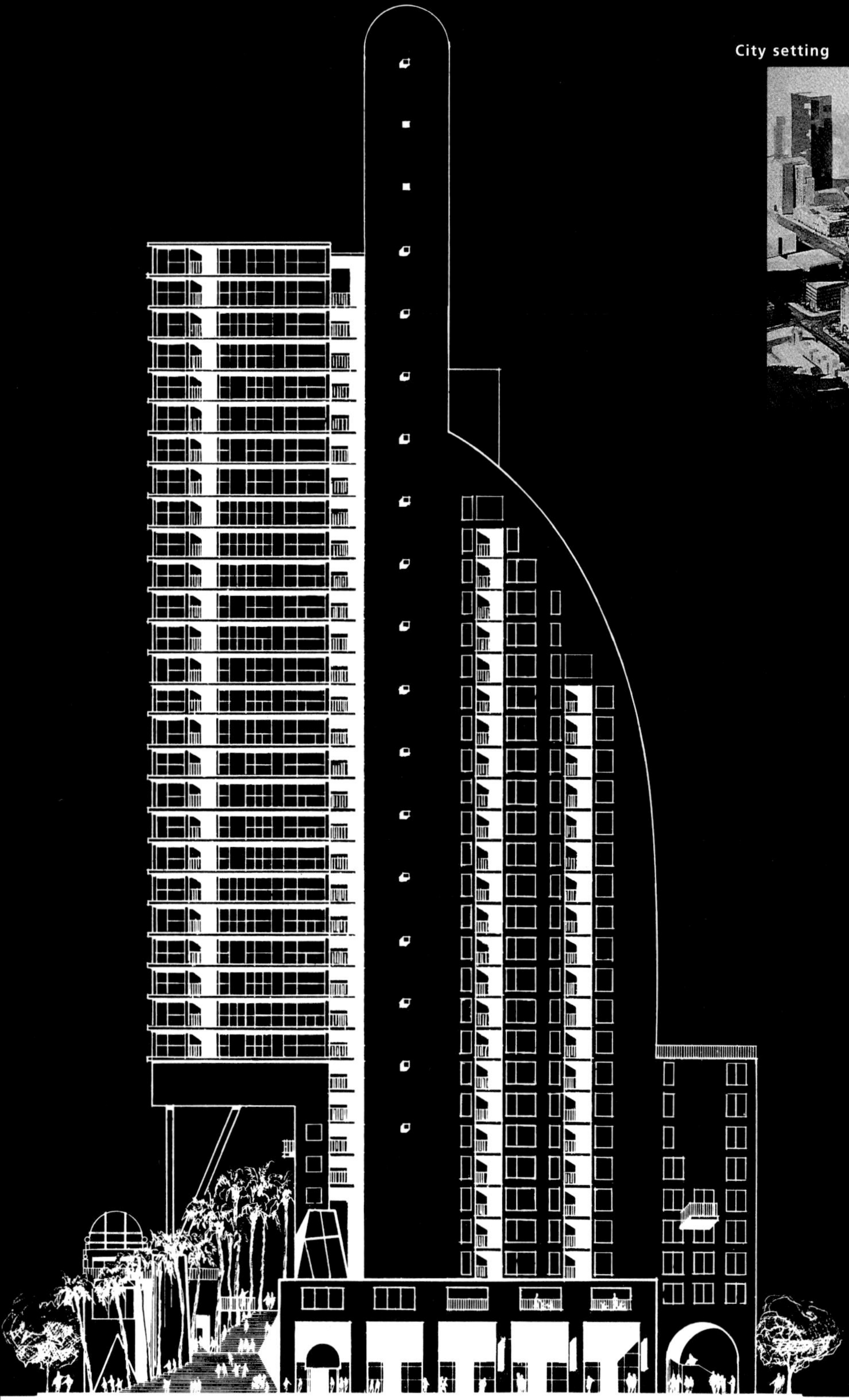

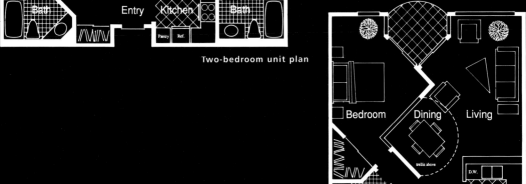

Two-bedroom unit plan

One-bedroom unit plan

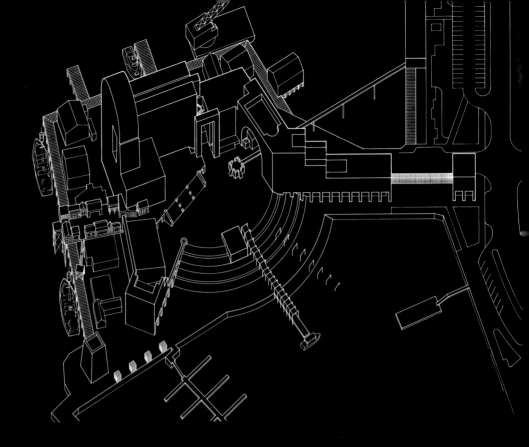

G Street Mole

Designed 1983

San Diego's downtown bayfront is the focus of a running battle perhaps best described as *The People v. The Port District.* The latter has jurisdiction over state-owned tidelands in five coastal cities. The parties wrangle over what constitutes public access to the waterfront, a right protected by California law.

Increasingly, visual and physical access to the waterfront is being blocked by large buildings and high-rise hotels developed mainly to satisfy the San Diego Unified Port District's mandate to generate revenue. Oddly, people-friendly parks and marinas along the waterfront—one of the city's chief assets and a year-round attraction—are maddeningly difficult to find behind a tall wall of tourist-oriented buildings. Ribbons of parkland with concrete paths lie between the bay and congested streets; piers for ferry boats, cruise ships, and United States Navy craft; rusty commercial shipyards and the like.

In 1983, the Port District sponsored a national design competition for a mole, or bulbous spit of land, to extend G Street into the bay. Quigley's team placed second in the competition. Their idea was to respect and recapture the salty character and appeal of a working port that existed alongside urban attractions, to give San Diego the large public gathering place it lacked, and to contribute adventure and zing to the city. The spirited proposal includes an outlandishly appealing pastiche of architectural styles at various scales. Among the amusements for fun and profit: an aquarium, an amphitheater that steps down into the water to allow wading, a movie theater, a 24-hour cafe and convenience store, a bank, and a children's museum.

In stark and smelly contrast to this recreation/entertainment zone, commercial fishing operations would continue unfettered on the mole's outer edge, off-limits to visitors but not beyond the sensory limit of their eyes and noses. A shantytown-style row of outdoor fish stands, a fish market, a fishing museum, and a chapel for blessing the tuna fleet balance the playground atmosphere of the mole and pay tribute to an important regional industry in decline. Changes in landscaping from low-level coastal desert plants to mountain pines mark the ascent to a sixteenth-floor observation deck.

Getting in and around the complex would be half the fun. Pedestrians would teeter across a narrow bridge, passing a colorful, bobbing "buoy museum" on their way to a bar with city and bay views. Performers would brighten office workers' lunch hours with music and dance on a sweeping plaza.

This could have been the novel and memorable development that San Diego craved as a bayfront signature. Instead, the Port District developed the mole with a seafood restaurant on the water, surrounded by green lawns and artfully placed trees, winding concrete walks, and vast

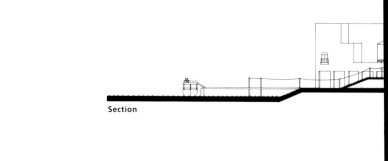

Section

◄─(N)   Site plan

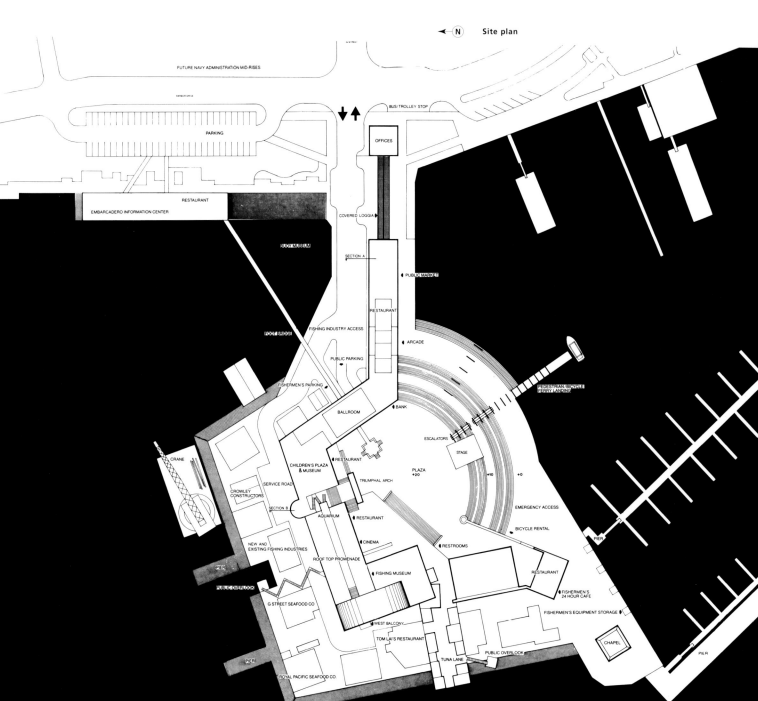

FUTURE NAVY ADMINISTRATION MID-RISES

G STREET

HARBOR DRIVE

PARKING

BUS/TROLLEY STOP

OFFICES

RESTAURANT

EMBARCADERO INFORMATION CENTER

COVERED LOGGIA

BUOY MUSEUM

SECTION A

PUBLIC MARKET

RESTAURANT

FOOT BRIDGE

FISHING INDUSTRY ACCESS

ARCADE

PUBLIC PARKING

PEDESTRIAN/BICYCLE
FERRY LANDING

FISHERMEN'S PARKING

BALLROOM

BANK

CRANE

ESCALATORS

STAGE

CHILDREN'S PLAZA
& MUSEUM

RESTAURANT

PLAZA
+20

+10   +0

CROWLEY
CONSTRUCTORS

SERVICE ROAD

TRIUMPHAL ARCH

SECTION B

EMERGENCY ACCESS

AQUARIUM

RESTAURANT

BICYCLE RENTAL

NEW AND
EXISTING FISHING INDUSTRIES

CINEMA

PIER

ROOF TOP PROMENADE

RESTAURANT

PIER

FISHING MUSEUM

RESTROOMS

RESTAURANT

PUBLIC OVERLOOK

FISHERMEN'S
24 HOUR CAFE

G STREET SEAFOOD CO

WEST BALCONY

FISHERMEN'S EQUIPMENT STORAGE

TOM LAI'S RESTAURANT

CHAPEL

PIER

TUNA LANE

PUBLIC OVERLOOK

PIER

ROYAL PACIFIC SEAFOOD CO.

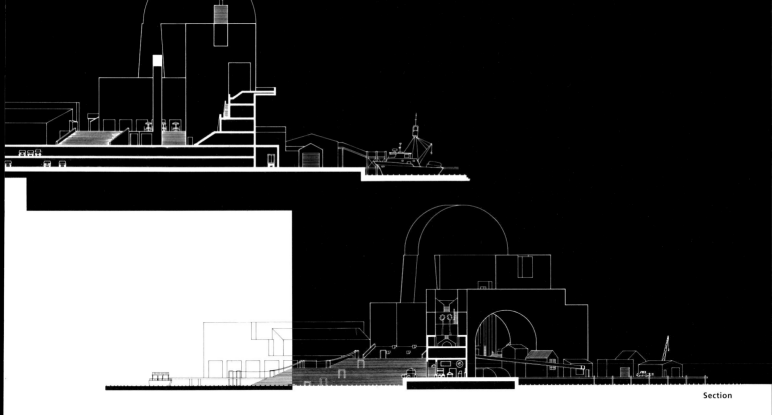

Section

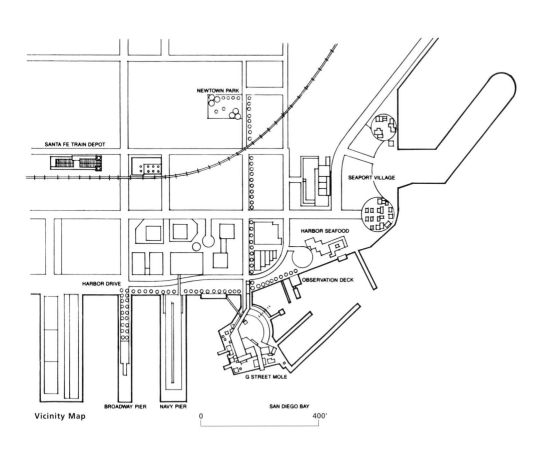

NEWTOWN PARK

SANTA FE TRAIN DEPOT

SEAPORT VILLAGE

HARBOR SEAFOOD

OBSERVATION DECK

HARBOR DRIVE

G STREET MOLE

BROADWAY PIER

NAVY PIER

SAN DIEGO BAY

Vicinity Map

0   400'

San Diego Municipal Gymnasium

Designed 1993–1994

For years, San Diego planners have eyed a prominent but deteriorating and crime-ridden downtown intersection, Twelfth Avenue and Broadway, as a possible site for an important civic building and urban-renewal catalyst.

Quigley, as design architect, with Wheeler Wimer Blackman & Associates, designed a people-friendly, street-smart municipal gymnasium and community park for this one-and-a-half-block site.

The 47,000-square-foot facility was to replace an old gym that is in constant use in nearby Balboa Park. By designing the new gym with an arcade and cafe that overlook the park, community rooms, and a walled "tot lot," Quigley offered a broader interpretation of the gymnasium as a community center.

The neighborhood, a crossroads at the heart of the city, would gain desperately needed public green space. Establishing a park along Twelfth Avenue would also contribute toward realizing a longstanding urban plan to transform Twelfth Avenue and other north-south streets into green boulevards connecting the city's finest natural assets, Balboa Park and San Diego Bay.

The park, designed by Martin Poirier of Andrew Spurlock Martin Poirier Landscape Architects in San Diego, includes meandering paths similar to those of a nearby college campus, trees planted for soft- or hard-edge definition, bocce courts, and a basketball court that doubles as an outdoor performance space with bleachers.

The glass-enclosed arcade, cafe, and elevator would be social magnets, strengthening security by keeping lots of watchful eyes on the street. Accessible by public transportation and open day and night, a busy gym would generate so much street activity that public fear of crime might justifiably recede.

Opposing the recommendations of the city redevelopment agency and virtually every community group involved, the city council decided to strip the redevelopment agenda from the project and move it to Balboa Park, where Quigley's revised version of the gym is under construction. The Twelfth Avenue and Broadway area has continued to decline.

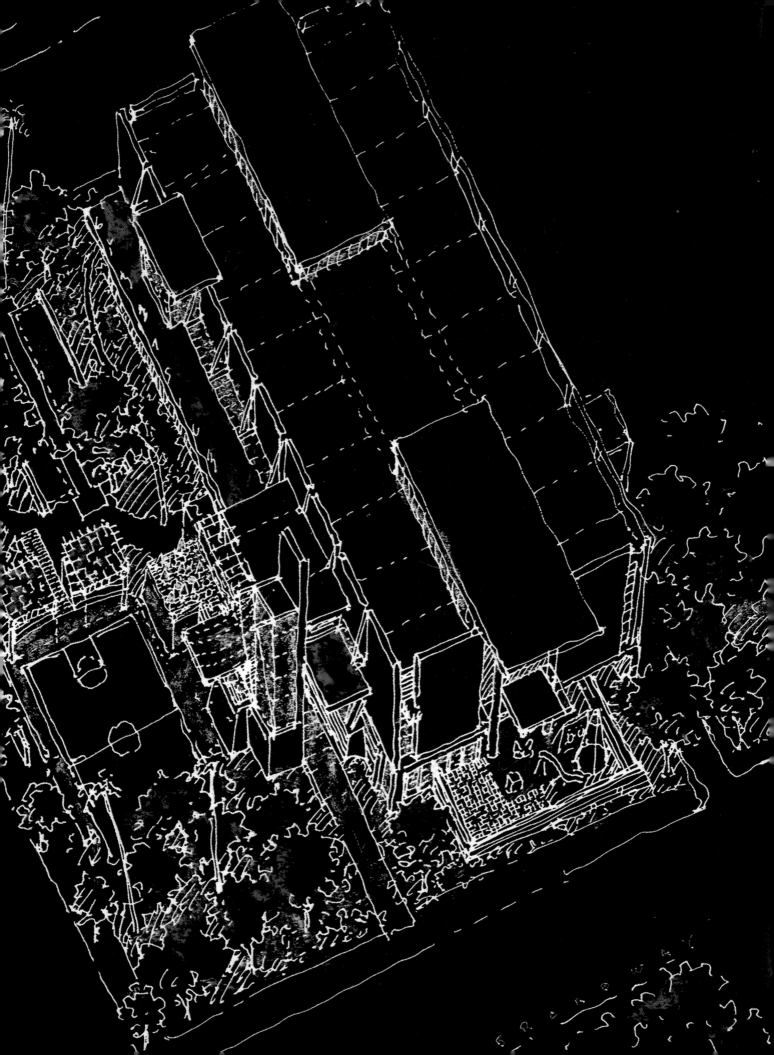

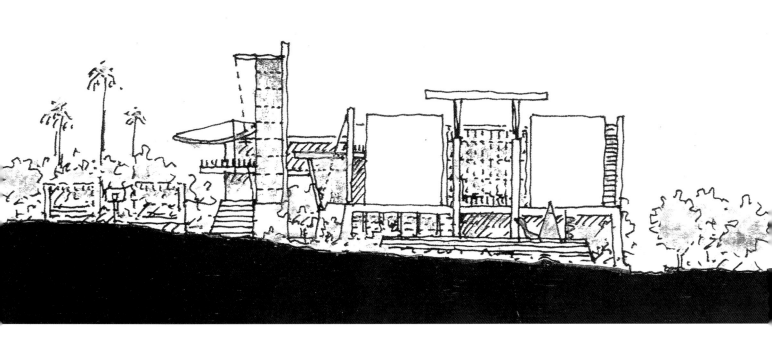

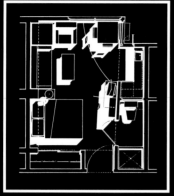

Room plan

Malibu Studio Hotel

Designed 1991-1992

Each of Quigley's four downtown SROs for low-income workers, displaced seniors, and homeless people in transition has improved on its predecessor, winning consistent praise for social responsiveness and awards for the architect, developers, and San Diego city government.

The Malibu—186 rooms around a landscaped courtyard—was to be the best, most homelike of the bunch. At an estimated cost of $45 per square foot, it would fill an oblong lot in Centre City East, a blighted, floundering, yet architecturally interesting part of downtown.

The Malibu would provide a much-needed neighborhood anchor and help jump-start the area's social life and economy. Like other Quigley designs for downtown, the Malibu would welcome the neighborhood into its corner deli/cafe and hide its parking garage underground. Inside, a community could take root as Malibu residents crossed paths in a common TV lounge, reading room (an amenity that other SRO residents had previously requested of Quigley), and furnished outdoor terraces.

Quigley views the Malibu room design as a breakthrough. His 14' x 18' floor plan functions and feels more like an apartment than a standard motel room. A small vestibule, a built-in storage column and nightstand between "bedroom" and "living room," a recessed kitchen, and different flooring material under the dining table are some of the devices that suggest an array of rooms within a single 252-square-foot room.

Windows on the world heighten a sense of spaciousness: there are large corner windows in the dining area and a centrally-located television set, the vital sign of many homes. The TV set can be swiveled toward the living, dining, or sleeping areas.

The proposed Malibu site remains vacant at this writing, although Quigley's ideas evolved into an SRO that is expected to be completed in Palo Alto, California, in 1996.

North elevation

'J' STREE

CLIPPED CEILING LINE

Section

M. F. & Ace Co. Building

Designed 1989

Conjuring a mythical past for a forlorn downtown site, Quigley designed a contemporary live/work loft building on the edge of the historic Gaslamp Quarter and adjacent to handsome old brick loft buildings now used commercially.

The architect fabricated a plausible name, The M. F. & Ace Co. Building, partly so residents would feel connected to a heritage of virtuous, if mysterious, labors. "People will ask what the M. F. & Ace Co. used to produce and thank you for saving the structure for reuse," Quigley predicted.

The seven-story project would be built of cast-in-place concrete. The regular geometry of the facades would give way to an interior plan made more habitable and interesting with angled and stepped corridor walls. Quigley's sculptural signature would rise on heavily traveled Market Street: a drum-shaped room crowned with a sun deck and one of the playful spires the architect favors.

Full-height industrial doors on each of the 87 high-ceilinged units would roll up to transform the flexible live/work spaces into airy, light-filled places. Sun decks, outdoor corridors and patios, and street-level gardens would invite sunlight and landscaping into a gritty corner of the city.

Like the Malibu Studio Hotel, this could have been an anchor project in a floundering area. Old loft buildings nearby have since been renovated successfully.

Quigley's client abandoned the proposal for financial reasons, leaving the block to deteriorate into vacant storefronts, a used restaurant-supply store and a large parking lot, coincidentally operated by Ace Parking, Inc.

Architect's Notes:

This project explores a new type of urban housing for downtown San Diego—contemporary live/work lofts. Loft living/working is more than high ceilings and factory sash. It is also more than a lifestyle. It has to do with elusive ideas of both community and history.

Old factory buildings were places of productivity and creativity. The employees had a common bond and purpose. Their buildings spoke to those needs in the form of simple and flexible production spaces punctuated by very specific spaces such as a public entry and product display space, the company cafeteria, and the executive block of offices.

The romance of loft living has to do with "fitting" into those places and with the energy generated by a group of buildings designed to produce a product. An oversized apartment building with high ceilings and nostalgic detailing is still an apartment building. The romance of loft living has to do with sensing an historical continuum and being a part of it.

Essays

In the last forty to fifty years, broad cultural and economic changes have affected the architecture profession in America. Cumulative, imperceptible on a day-to-day basis, no one architect or firm can do much about them; yet the challenges they pose to architecture as an artistic and socially altruistic enterprise are enormous.

In the ten years between 1975 and 1985, the number of registered architects in the United States as a fraction of the population more than doubled. The profession has continued to grow at this pace into the 1990s. This would be acceptable if the national building economy were growing at a similar pace, but it is not. The portion of the Gross Domestic Product (GDP) accounted for by building construction has been dropping steadily for decades. Also, although subject to roughly an eight-year boom-and-bust cycle, the average number of square feet built per year has risen very little. Put these numbers together and what do we have overall? More and more architects fussing over relatively fewer square feet on paper and, perhaps more important, over relatively cheaper square feet on the ground. With notable exceptions, Americans en masse have decided for decades that making and enjoying fine buildings is worth less time and money than making and enjoying other fine things, such as ever more sophisticated movies, music, medical care, weapons, cars, clothes, sports equipment, communication systems, real estate deals, and financial instruments.

Economy,

Architecture, and

While construction has continued to slip as a portion of the GDP, the real estate and finance sectors have grown. More buildings than ever today, including houses, are being built speculatively and/or commercially for sale, resale, and rental income. Such buildings are means rather than ends—means, specifically, of making money for their titular owners and for the people who finance them. Such buildings are engines of wealth-creation—dollar locomotives, nothing more—and the less they cost to build, the better. This fact about contemporary building is perfectly well-known to architects. Yet they are bound, both ethically and professionally, to view buildings as ends in themselves, or as means to the ultimate end of making better lives for a broad constituency: the public, the man-in-the-street, the building's users or inhabitants, the citizens and dwellers of the future.

Architects, of course, are not the only professionals to succumb to the logic of the marketplace: lawyers did long ago; doctors are next; engineers can't see what the problem is. But matters are worse for architects because most buildings are not private goods; they are inherently what economists call "public goods" (or "bads"), objects from which the public cannot be excluded, and that cannot themselves be shielded from the public's use and appreciation. Buildings leap past their lot lines, broadcasting themselves into the ether of the city like soundless radios that cannot be turned off, entering the minds and lives of people who are completely innocent of their design, construction, and reasons for being.

Situated at the geographical and historical front line that is Southern California, Rob Quigley has responded to these concerns with the remarkable energy and ethicality that make him the signal architect he is today. In a 1991 article in *Architecture California*, reprinted in this volume, Quigley outlines what he calls "six contradictions" that inform the regional and cultural context of his work: the conflict between transience and permanence in habitation; the need for both community and privacy that is fostered by electronic communication; the clash of liberal and conservative political ideals that surround the act of building; the interrelationship of work and leisure in today's economy; the increasingly multicultural, multiethnic nature of society in America; and the contest between respect for nature and climate and the liberation from them that technology offers. Quigley's optimism shines through every word; a true entrepreneur, he sees opportunity in every problem. In view of what has happened to American architecture in the latter half of this century and of what it will face at the turn of the millennium, Quigley's struggle to make a living and to make genuinely humane architecture, of his time and place, shines all the brighter.

Let me return to the growth and democratization of the architecture profession. While it is true that once architectural practitioners and building tradespersons did not require lengthy educations and professional titles, today, by and large, they do. This would account for some of the recent growth in the number of architects as distinct from builders/draftspersons. But one look at how quickly they are adopting Computer Aided Design (CAD) ought to give us pause. For from a rational, economic point of view, the productivity of an architect/draftsperson using CAD correctly can be roughly double that of one using a drawing board.

Quigley

Michael Benedikt

This has profound implications for design, for the kinds of buildings that will be built. The point to be made is this: When architecture firms compete with one another—as they must under constant government and market pressure to lower their fees—and use CAD to do so, we can expect considerably more unemployment for tomorrow's architects and draftspeople.

How has Quigley responded to this "rationalization"? He is adopting CAD slowly, careful to use it to improve productivity not by keeping staff levels down, but by augmenting services to offer better drawings, better accounting, better specifications, and more flexibility—not at reduced fees, but at the same fees or higher. But in a more general sense, and in response to the democratization of the profession,

Quigley is committed to finding new things for architects to do

Alden House

and new ways for them to operate: becoming directly involved in the lives and aspirations of local communities, taking risks with new building types such as the private/public SRO hotels illustrated in this book, refining commercial construction techniques such as site-cast tilt-up walls for structures like his Sherman Heights Community Center, and conceptual programming of hybrid public/private projects such as his rapid transit concept plan for the city of San Bruno, California. Quigley also takes care to present himself as neither the clever architect-of-independent-means nor the humble builder/architect-of-the-people, neither the suited architect of blue-chip corporations nor the hip-pocket architect of commercial developers. Rather, he is unique: a casual yet dogged, experienced yet always-young architect and sometime college teacher, just as capable of award-winning stylistic flourishes as of cut-to-the-chase frugality, a person entirely realistic about what can be done, when, and for whom, with no apparent bitterness, and indeed, with an enviable joie de vivre.

This, then, is Quigley's implicit advice to young architects:

Work, if you can, only for individuals, communities, and institutions. Better yet: Work openly with the people who will use the building. No stealth. Make yourself "inedible" to developers, large corporations, and bankers. This can be said even though Quigley's four built SRO hotels were the result of developers' entrepreneurship, because the way these buildings were funded, designed, and even conceived remained thoroughly civic-minded. These SROs are gifts to their streets. They lend dignity to a community that would otherwise be all but homeless; they revitalize the city; they are a source of pride for those who were involved in their creation as well as for those who were not. The design of each new SRO project was thoroughly informed by communication with the users of the preceding one. Precious few buildings are refined in this way by their architects.

Another consequence of the economic pressures under which architecture is practiced today is the continuing drive to find, use, and dignify lighter, faster, and cheaper methods and materials of construction. In this regard California leads the nation if not the developed world, and we find Quigley at the (budget-) cutting edge.

What else is an architect to do while he waits for the client with a limitless budget, boundless courage, and impeccable taste? Economic forces are tidal. Indeed, the reason that the modern movement and, specifically, the International Style, swept the world in less than twenty years had little or nothing to do with generally received notions of rationality and hygiene; the beauty of precision, openness, and abstraction; or new social-democratic projects made possible by rational engineering, teamwork, and new materials. Europe between the wars was financially ruined; thin, stuccoed, metal-windowed, modernist boxes were simply cheaper and quicker to build.

But developers, realtors, bankers, and landowners—not to mention the governments here and in Europe—were quick to see the opportunities for profit that opened up with cheaper space, higher densities, and rising land prices. While architects cultivated the company of modern painters, musicians, and dancers; played with color and planes and "exploded

**Sherman Heights
Community Center**

**Sherman Heights
Community Center**

space" and generally outdid one another in revolutionary rectitude; persuaded themselves of the charms of raw concrete and the efficiency of curtain walls; and sold off—no, gave away—everything technical and quantitative about buildings to the engineers; the realtors, developers, and landowners laughed their way to the proverbial bank.

With every passing year architects' cost ceilings were lowered. Under the delusion that "less is more" and that their creative genius was at stake in triumphantly meeting tighter budgets, architects perceived only one way out: to continue to mortgage tradition, to drain away the material content of buildings and with it the expensive demands of craft and labor. So, today, in the land of freeways and loops, we have stucco, gypsum board, wood frame, aluminum windows, concrete, a few improbable shapes here and gay colors there, low ceilings everywhere, feathery steel and glass boxes, signs and boards propped from behind, wires against the sky: architecture as hunger art, architects as hunger artists.

Quigley, like all contemporary architects, has not been immune to these trends. With construction materials at hand, he strives to make a good impression, rescuing what he can of Southern California's regional taste in forms and colors. Valiantly, at the Sherman Heights Community Center, he tried to find the beauty in tilt-up concrete construction, but "vertical gardens" along the walls will, probably wisely, cover much of it. From his houses to his churches and community and mixed-use buildings, Quigley's architecture deftly recovers the formal possibilities remaining to architects under the new construction regime of the quick and cheap.

Indeed, he makes these recoveries seem easy, more like happy discoveries.

But in truth, architecture of the past century, of the sort we admire in Europe and even in North and Central America—a materially crafted architecture nourished by generous capital investment, that actually improved on rather than merely quoted the region's climate- and material-driven history, that was a public-spirited gift rather than a burden to future generations—is hardly possible anymore. Instead, we have become specialists in expressing the exuberance of cheapness and consumption blossoming in the desert at the confluence of rivers of money. That Quigley can lend dignity to the architecture of our times—to my mind in its death throes as a material art—is high achievement indeed.

Two other major social changes continue to demand and receive architectural responses.

One is the often-noted takeover of the landscape by the automobile. The other is the rapid rise of information, entertainment, and communication technologies in the last ten to twenty years. A few remarks about these two factors will inform the reader of the importance of Quigley's search for solutions.

Every architect in America must make his peace with a future predicated on the needs of the automobile, and once again, the architects of Southern California lead the way. The ground is hard in San Diego; for the most part, its landscape elements are not mesa and swale, but curb and lane, overpass and underpass. The sky is large. Here and there palm trees and eucalyptus sway like survivors of a passing asphalt machine. Roadside brush awaits its turn to be cleared for a higher purpose.

While one might expect a golf clubhouse to be well-appointed and landscaped (see Quigley's Tustin Ranch Clubhouse, p. 78), we might not expect the same of a quasi-urban, very low budget community center. But Quigley insists: nature shall have its place. The postage-stamp-sized grounds of the Sherman Heights Community Center are mostly garden by design, continuing right up the walls and on every balustrade, as in Mexico.

Quigley is characteristically Californian in his acceptance, even embrace, of the automobile. His SROs, however, provide far fewer parking spaces than the city normally requires for their density. Quigley showed that these requirements were unreasonable for the buildings' intended use, and they were waived. Nevertheless, some parking was required, and at 202 Island Inn, for example, Quigley seizes the point of descent to and ascent from the underground parking to create a public entry space. The streetscapes of our new downtowns are ruined by parking garage entrances, those roaring dark holes to basements that empty cars onto side streets. It's enough to make one long for jammed, on-street parking, jaywalking pedestrians, bicyclists dodging diesel trucks, dogs among the shoppers, and a bit of yelling … in short, for a Manhattan, Mexico City, or Johannesburg street. I think Quigley would agree.

We turn to the effect of the media.

Where are you when you are on the phone? Watch a person using a cellular phone as he or she ambles down the sidewalk or sits grinning on a bench, waving an arm, obviously entertained—see the faraway look in the eyes, those out-of-sync expressions. Come out of a movie matinee. Where are you? Where have you been?

**Tustin Ranch Clubhouse
and Community Center**

Put on a Walkman—the whole world instantly becomes a movie, complete with soundtrack, in which you, the audience, happen to be able to bump into the things you view. Take the headphones off and the angels vanish. The world suddenly looks and sounds like the boring, grating place it always was.

Crank up that radio in your car; fill your head with Rush Limbaugh or the Grateful Dead; make it a concert hall on wheels, with buttons to adjust reverberation for jazz club, stadium, or den.

And how nice must your living place be if you have cable television with a hundred channels available at the touch of your thumb? Before long, virtual reality will be real(ity), a city will squeeze onto a CD-ROM, you will have eyes around the world, while the reality of your room will dwindle to a chair, a bed, a tangle of wires, and some half-eaten food.

In short, this is not a world receptive to architecture the way it is taught to architects. This is not Haussmann's Paris; this is not Rome or Helsinki. It is William Gibson's Sprawl, a vast decaying Chinatown with cyberspace coming in through the cracks.

Hardly any architect practicing today is more aware of the impact of the entertainment and media industries on our physical culture than Quigley, working where Los Angeles meets the Mexican border, where the Arcadian Dream has so recently run out of steam. Perhaps because his youthful experiences in the Peace Corps lent a realist and populist cast to his thinking, Quigley has chosen a most difficult course. On the one hand, he must make public buildings that are striking on the ground, buildings that somehow demonstrate a mongrel order, a readiness—or rather, happiness—to serve all comers with an egalitarianism not unlike television, reaching out for a broad audience with strong, workable imagery. On the other hand, he must please the gods of architecture, who are protective of what Louis Kahn called Order. Moreover, Quigley is committed to entering the life of a community and of his clients. As one not quite among them, he seeks the political, financial, and aesthetic grounds on which they can come together around a particular building design, a real place, distracted though they may be by the seductive call to immersion in the mediaverse. No single force usurps attention to the physical world like the collective electronic media; no single trend is more threatening to architecture, especially, in the long run, architecture that would accommodate and appease it.

Video Porch
La Jolla Museum of Contemporary Art

This, then, summarizes a bleaker view of architecture's condition and the hopefulness of Quigley's contribution. This book presents the work of a remarkable architect tackling democratic architecture at the turn of this century with far more optimism than I could muster here, writing in his honor.

Driving through the exurban continuum that fills much of America today

is an exercise in avoidance. Everything is kept at bay: other drivers, the weather, confrontation with potential intruders into shopping and living compounds, and a sense of place or nature. One glides through this scenery lulled by the smoothness of selling and the safety of mediocrity. The culture of avoidance and fear has created a suburban landscape nurtured by mass production and given a new face by image-manipulation technology.[1] What escapes notice is the reality of construction: how something was made, of what, where, by and for whom, and who controls it. Rob Wellington Quigley's architecture responds to this situation through articulation that makes the structure of our society visible in construction itself.

This is not a new strategy in architecture, and much of what is fascinating about Quigley's work derives from its recognizability. Quigley creates in the tradition of California's Spanish-revival mission style, building on a foundation of standardized construction methods and collective imagery developed in tandem with these methods. This does not mean that he merely employs a particular aesthetic, but rather that he picks up on a particular warping of styles to create forms that are logical and relevant and so reveal their history and place.[2]

The culture of avoidance and an architecture of articulation are intimately connected. Both evidence the idea of openness and fluidity that appeared with modernization in the United States and with the development of American cultural attitudes toward space. By the late nineteenth

Clarity
and the Culture of

century, the great route west was dotted with wooden balloon-frame houses in gridded settlements. Semiskilled craftsmen could assemble these structures in a short time, making them available to

people in a wide range of socioeconomic groups.[3] Thrown up using standardized construction techniques, they allowed flexibility for changing uses while presenting a facade (and often not much more than that) of order and propriety borrowed from the high-culture lexicon of architecture written back East. Stick-style and shingle-style houses simultaneously represented and utilized America's great timber resources as they evidenced the freedom with which this self-made society created its own spaces and rituals of use.

This was democratic architecture: It made the emblems of power (symmetry, columns, parlors) available to nearly everyone, and its system of many interdependent parts contrasted sharply with the hierarchical formal traditions of Italian and French architecture. It also created each house as a reproducible unit that, while perhaps indistinguishable from its neighbor and continually in transition, established a self-contained place of domestic order as a counterpoint to nature and society outside, which were often perceived as inimical.[4]

Sherman Heights Community Center

By the time this building tradition reached California, it had reached the limits of its viability. Wood was not plentiful in Southern California; the climate did not demand the condensed, vertical, closed-in structures of the Northeast; and the logic of land occupation was different in this semiarid place of latifundios. As a result, the stick and shingle styles merged with existing Mexican architectural traditions—a blend of Spanish abstract ordering devices and local responses to climate, building materials, and geography—and adapted the open model of the Indian bungalow. The mission style thus emerged as a hybrid construction of solid walls, sheltered courtyards, isolated decorative elements, and a still-articulated wood skeleton that tied all of these pieces together and maintained a sense of civic propriety.

This solution was not limited to historicist modes: It also describes the twentieth-century residential work of Irving Gill, Rudolph M. Schindler at Pueblo Ribera and Kings Road in Los Angeles, and Frank Gehry at his own house in Santa Monica. It also underlies the vernacular of the tract house and the tilt-up commercial building, though here the structural skeleton is often repressed as a result of the public's increasingly paranoid attitudes toward legibility and engagement. The combined requirements of air-conditioning, building codes, privacy, and mass-marketing have led to the creation of smooth white walls and ceilings that hide all signs of structural and mechanical elements. Today the skeleton appears only in the surrounding ubiquitous billboards, telephone wires, traffic signs, and highway infrastructure that we do not usually consider part of the architectural tradition.[5]

Avoidance

Aaron Betsky

What is lost in this contemporary scene is a sense of communal action. This, however, was never a strong part of the American building tradition, which de-emphasizes civic monumentality in favor of the individual. Instead, in the United States it is the collage of individual constructed expression, whether "Painted Ladies" in San Francisco or skyscrapers in New York, that creates a sense of the democratic city. In Southern California, the architecture of the commercial strip, the suburban residential development, and the edge-city cluster of office buildings, apartments, and shopping malls represents the region's communal ethos. It is clear that here the desire to build a better place, to engage with others and with one's surroundings, and to nourish a culture of different classes, races, and sexes, has been replaced precisely by the avoidance of such efforts.

Rob Wellington Quigley's architecture explodes under these conditions. Based on expression rather than repression, it makes clear the everyday connections that create a building and resurrects an earlier building tradition whose pale reflection now covers the seas of anonymous developments in which Quigley finds himself working.

I first came across Quigley's work in his 1983 Jaeger Beach House in Del Mar, a little compound wedged between the beach and the highway. Here Quigley turned the defensive walls of its neighbors into an opportunity to create reflective Japanese spaces at the base, a maze of concrete block. Rising above this inward-turned world is an assortment of rambling spaces that quote, often quite literally, turn-of-the-century bungalows as well

Linda Vista Library

as mission-style protective elements. It is a rambling assemblage in which each piece reveals snippets of the whole.

The civic equivalent to this domestic prism is the 1987 Linda Vista Library, a concrete-block addendum to a shopping center. It has the same abstracted, mission-style arches and massive walls undercut by low openings as its neighbors, but here the pieces are incomplete, thin, and layered. The complexity of the structure speaks through the composition, the grandeur of its calling through the main facade. These articulations would never exist in the value-engineered world of "civic facilities." But the real payoff (to use the language of such a world) is inside, where massive wood trunks and laminated truss branches punctuate a soaring, loftlike space. These trees of knowledge are purely structural, yet their elaboration and active composition belie the simplicity of their function.

Even more remarkable than in these projects—a signature home for a well-off client, and a moment of civic exuberance (whose construction, in any case, probably would no longer be possible in an era in which the state of California spends more on prisons than on education)—is Quigley's ability to create passages of articulation in such humble, low-budget structures as single room occupancy hotels. In a series of SROs that Quigley designed during the 1980s in downtown San Diego, he created facades that responded to their surroundings, crystallizing legible order out of the jumble of commercial buildings on the site.

Once again, the true achievements are inside. There, squeezing through the security areas and the condensed private spaces, winding past the despair that usually fills such spaces, are corridors that allow one to see and understand the major constructional, spatial, and functional elements of the hotels. Structural gymnastics are not evident here, only the clear use of post and beam and the placement of skylights, windows, and clerestories to map nodes of activity within the space and to draw one through it. Quigley used the complexities of site and function to reveal the contradictory economic, social, and physical pressures as they become built artifacts in and of themselves.

Quigley has continued to use such techniques of expressive assemblage in a variety of settings, from the pared-down shelters of the Escondido Transit Center to the elaborate stew of forms that make up the large private houses he has recently completed in Telluride, Colorado, and San Juan Capistrano, California. In the works are further developments of this style, as in the Solana Beach Transit Station. Here, echoes of the work of Irving Gill and the stations of the Santa Fe Railroad coexist with the earthworks of any infrastructure project and with a hybrid collection of traditional facades and a shopping arcade.

One of the most interesting of Quigley's recent projects is the Sherman Heights Community Center. Sited in a predominantly Hispanic neighborhood, this is the "big house" meant to consolidate the activities of a community defending itself against rampant commercialism and its disruptive social consequences. To accomplish this, Quigley reduced the main message to two icons: a sheltering roof, as large as any shingle-style gesture, that towers over and shades everything within its reach; and a garden denoting this site as a special precinct. Eastern and Hispanic building traditions thus meet in their most condensed form, and Quigley creates not so much a set of usable spaces as a collection of fragmentary enclosures, free-flowing spaces, and points of shelter. He uses what is by now his recognizable vocabulary of tilt-up concrete slab surfaces, wood trellises cantilevered or splayed from the main body of the building, roofs and walls separated by open spaces or clerestories, and massive columns supporting laminated beams that tie these pieces together with heavy metal sockets.

Sherman Heights Community Center

The result is a completely active space. What is missing is as important as what one can see. There is only generic space that is almost completely contiguous with the exterior. There are no direct quotations, though there is a sense of familiarity about the whole building. There is no hierarchical, monumental composition, though this is clearly a civic place. There is no attempt to create either a pure order or an allusive response to a commercial environment.

Instead, there is articulation. Everywhere one turns in a Quigley-designed building, things are clear. As in a bungalow or the steel-frame buildings of the Chicago School, structure becomes the experiential framework that allows one to place oneself in the world. This is true also for the sequence of spaces he reveals through the layering of light and for the quotations of fragmentary orders that allude to greater and more abstract structures. Articulate architecture has become a clear style that works.

At times these articulations become rhetorical, as in the shading devices and columns that fill Quigley's recent buildings, the trees of knowledge, the sailing roof, or the many and often perhaps redundant porticoes. If so, it is because they are shouting into the wind. The notion of architecture promoting clarity and understanding is not popular, either in the academy, where it is suspect because a subjective voice can be seen as an articulation of power of which the architect is not even aware,[6] or with the general public, who sees architecture as a luxury that is only part of a broader culture industry. The profession, meanwhile, has usually responded to these two perceptions by calling on history, codes, or confusing theories to help create diluted reflections of its own building practices.

Yet Quigley is not alone in his practice. He is one of a group of architects working mainly in the Southwest and West who are gathering an understanding of vernacular, stylistic precedent, the "second nature" of codes that define much of the landscape,[7] and the dissipative character of our urban landscape to create forms that do not contain the forces at work here, but rather articulate them in an attempt at civic understanding.[8] The work of such practitioners as Koning Eizenberg, Franklin D. Israel, Mehrdad Yazdani, and Patkau Architects is hard to classify ideologically, but each architect or firm shares a desire to make real places of connection and legibility and collages of order.

This does not mean that these architects constitute a school or movement. Most of them, including Quigley, would not classify themselves with one another and might view their allegiances as closer to that of designers whose work does not display such concerns for a humble making of civic spaces. Quigley himself points out that his work is more concerned with fusing vernacular building methods with an eclectic use of styles and construction elements.[9] To an outside observer, however, what ties this work together is a sense of appropriateness or fit. It does not rely on forms or materials outside the communities in which it appears or offer alternatives to that world. It does not tower over or seek to burrow underneath the structures of everyday life, yet neither is it an anonymous architecture that seeks to disappear into the self-organizing structures of the modern metropolis.[10]

There is, in fact, an aesthetic to this work. I would call it Home Depot Modern. The work not only follows the same logic that goes into constructing each megalithic tilt-up hardware store of the Home Depot chain, but is made out of the pieces and parts that one can buy at any of these stores. Quigley does not let the pieces alone, but rather transforms them as a designer. This is where architecture—the self-consciousness about building—comes in: it is a low-tech version of technological expressionism (another Southern California architect, Craig Hodgetts, has referred to it as "raiding the parts bin") that in its methods of assemblage is nevertheless conscious of the culture of avoidance that usually denies the ways in which buildings are made out of these raw materials. The work of Rob Wellington Quigley and his fellow articulators opposes this "dumbness of construction" with a critical awareness of the contradictions and experiences that make up what Thom Mayne of Morphosis has called the "tension and risk" of urban life.

There is a beauty to Home Depot Modern, though it is not one that catches the eye with sensuality. (Even Quigley admits a certain wariness about the parts, preferring to think that the elements of his buildings come from other, more conventionally architectural sources.) Rather, it is a beauty that pushes normal forms to the breaking point, so the parts imply completion without drowning their own clarity in that wholeness. It is the beauty of towering tilt-up walls rising to premade trusses proliferating under skylights, and it is the wonder of the seemingly infinite perspective that opens up between the shelves of gadgets and gewgaws available to the American consumer.

Linda Vista Library

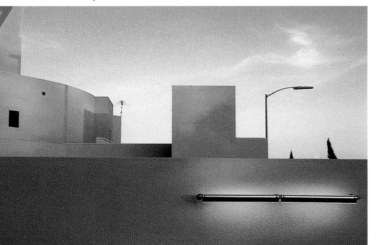

The specificity of the connections, the compositional skill, and the scale of the pieces make this work so wonderfully. Without that structural clarity, steeped in historic precedent and building practices but unjustified and glorious in its excess, these would be just buildings. With it, they are architecture.

A coda is necessary to any understanding of Quigley's work. As an architect who worked with the Peace Corps in Chile and lives and labors in a community increasingly dominated by Hispanic influences, Quigley responds to and seeks to express a fundamental cultural shift in the United States. Just as one might speculate how our English-language-dominant culture will withstand a demographic shift that will give this country's most populous states a Spanish-speaking majority within the next decade, so must one wonder whether the built environment will continue to repress the spatial traditions of diverse cultures in architectural "straitjackets" that follow a strictly Anglo continuum.[11]

Granted, a visit to Mexico shows that cities there have Wal-Marts too, and that strip culture thrives beyond the shantytowns. Yet just as the high-modernist vocabulary of much of Mexico's business districts has a particular cast that, ironically, brings it closer to Le Corbusier's early ideal of a participatory modernism,[12] so the ordinary architecture south of the U.S. border has an incompleteness, messiness, and adaptability unseen in the commercial areas. It also has a sensitivity to place, climate, and culture that was never a strong part of the American architectural tradition, but is now resurrecting itself in humble buildings and appropriate technologies.[13]

The architecture of Rob Wellington Quigley will have to articulate the hybrid culture that is seeping ever further north through the fences of the U.S. Border Patrol and across the mesas of San Diego County. Given his ability to respond to and clarify the reality of that county, there is every reason to believe that Quigley will find a place among those who seek to build a new, more vibrant culture out of the ruins of the culture of avoidance. Quigley's architecture stands as an unfinished monument to the desire to articulate.

1 This culture of fear has become the focus of a group of theoreticians and critics working in Southern California, who are erecting a countermyth to the traditional notion of a neo–Mediterranean paradise that has so long characterized public perception of the region. See in particular Mike Davis, *Beyond Blade Runner: Urban Control, The Ecology of Fear* (Westfield, NJ: Open Media, 1992), and Steven Flusty, *Building Paranoia: The Proliferation of Interdictory Space and the Erosion of Spatial Justice* (West Hollywood, CA: Los Angeles Forum for Architecture and Urban Design, 1994). The notion that architecture and design can smooth over and hide the reality of social injustice or unrest was first advanced by Jeffrey L. Meikle in *Twentieth Century Limited: Industrial Design in America, 1925–1939* (Philadelphia: Temple University Press, 1979); see in particular p. 170.

2 The notion of style has had negative connotations since the advent of modernism, as it was seen as an artificial imposition that covered the reality of construction. More recently, however, we have come to realize that style can also be seen as the representation of a particular perspective, sense of place, or critical stance. Style can be more than the appropriation of particular historical models: it can be a way of dressing, behaving, and belonging.

3 Vincent Scully, *The Shingle Style and the Stick Style* (New Haven, CT: Yale University Press, 1955).

4 For the use of interiors as places of cultural definition, see Mario Praz, *An Illustrated History of Interior Decoration from Pompeii to Art Nouveau* (London: Thames and Hudson, 1981), and Harvey Green, *The Light of the Home: An Intimate View of the Lives of Women in Victorian America* (New York: Pantheon Books, 1983).

5 Aaron Betsky, "The Wall, the Skeleton, the Road: Architecture in Southern California," *de Architect*, September 1994: 12–18.

6 For a concise compendium of essays on this theory, see Beatriz Colomina, ed., *Sexuality & Space* (New York: Princeton Architectural Press, 1992). See also Victor Burgin, "Geometry and Abjection," *AA Files*, no.15 (Summer 1988): 35–41; Laura Mulvey, "Visual Pleasure and Narrative Cinema," in her *Visual and Other Pleasures* (Bloomington, IN: Indiana University Press, 1989), 14–26.

7 This is a topic that deserves much more attention than it has received from critics. It has been broached most insistently by J.B. Jackson, starting with an interview in the *AIA Journal*, May 1982: 205–206.

8 This position is being developed by Margaret Crawford and John Kaliski at the Southern California Institute of Architecture. Basing their work on both the Situationist movement of the 1960s and the theories of Kevin Lynch, they are developing an "aesthetics of poverty" that offers an alternative to current "top–down" urban planning.

9 Rob Wellington Quigley, conversation with the author, February 23, 1995. This work has obvious roots not only in the work of Frank Gehry, but also more particularly in that of Charles and Ray Eames.

10 This is another currently fashionable architectural theory, which holds that any imposition of form must be avoided and that what is needed instead is a tracing of the already existing forms of the city. Thus architecture would be, in the words of New York-based architect Greg Lynn, an "unfolding of the site."

11 This trend has been pursued by the artists' and architects' collective Adobe LA through photographs, collages, and installations that seek to express the emergence of a counterculture with Hispanic roots.

12 For a discussion of Le Corbusier's "progressive" tendencies, see Manfredo Tafuri, *Architecture and Utopia: Design and Capitalist Development*, translated by Barbara Luigia La Penta (Cambridge, MA: MIT Press, 1979 [1973]).

13 This sensitivity has been charted by Richard Rodriguez in his *Days of Obligation: An Argument with My Mexican Father* (New York: Viking Press, 1992).

Framing

Rob Wellington Quigley

the Fit

Architecture can be seen as a set of simple and sometimes amusing paradoxes.

For instance, what relevance does an architecture of "permanence" have in an essentially transient society? Or "timelessness" in a society that values economic short-term gain above all else, "identity" in an era of instant global communication, or "spirituality" in a society that defines responsibility as nothing more than "on time and on budget"? What is the relevance of "craft" in a world that considers time-consuming care a luxury and haste a virtue?

While these may seem discouraging thoughts to some, they are the kinds of questions that have energized the work of my studio from the beginning and seem more relevant than ever today, as the architecture profession and educators begin to acknowledge that architects are badly out of sync with this society.

My early work focused overtly on four areas of concern:

Culture: Challenged by assertions from Chilean architects that this country had produced only one or two authentically "American" architects, I became interested in a celebration of a local architecture—localism understood not as an end in itself but as a means of transcending provincialism. Instead of accepting the traditional Eurocentric bias of American architecture, I felt that looking to the South and West would better enrich my particular cultural reality and opportunities.

Environment: The first oil embargo in the 1970s focused our work on the lost relationship between design and climate. Incorporated into a number of experimental houses in California and Japan, energy-efficient, passive design evolved from a polemical technique into an intrinsic part of the office's design process. Happily, after some years during which the profession drifted back to a cosmetically driven aesthetic, design with climate in mind is once again politically correct.

Context: We thought of context as more than the formal quality of the street or texture of the neighborhood: it was also the telephone poles and hamburger stands. Inspiration should literally come from the backyard next door. Light wood frame and stucco are the only "real materials" for our time and place—steel, brick, and stone are Eurocentric and elitist. Several projects explored alternative ways of ordering architecture. Beaux-Arts and modernist Cartesian grids were forsaken for collage or literary narratives as form-giving armature.

Culture: Sayer Beach House

Technology: Medieval attitudes about construction technology as handcraft (still very popular among the avant-garde today) are wonderfully romantic but clearly foreign to building as it is practiced in this country. The high-tech industrial methods envisioned by the early modernists are still largely irrelevant outside the theoretical world. We have focused on a different kind of craft—a craft to eliminate craft. Rather than subvert the conventional way of building and detailing, the architect instead should embrace and co-opt the status quo. Much of our work attempted to create architecture from the local wood-frame vernacular by understanding, prodding, and extending it rather than perverting it.

While we continue to explore and refine these concerns, **our current practice focuses more wholly on a single issue that lacked relevance in the earlier years.** That issue is the relationship of the practice of architecture to our broader society, or what might be called "fit."

Historically, lack of fit was not always a problem. Before the advent of modernism, for instance, the architecture of public buildings was in agreement with public expectation. No one had to ask which building was the library or the city hall. The Industrial Revolution and modernism challenged the validity of that agreement but (except for the fit between modernism and corporate buildings) were unable to produce a convincing substitute. Postmodernism's attempt to fill the void has proven largely superficial. Current experiments in deconstruction are provocative and in some cases important, but generally signal a retreat to the sanctuary of the fine arts.

My focus on the fit is driven not by theoretical or polemical interests but by raw fear of survival.

It has to be clear to any practicing architect that ours has become a profession in confrontation with those we profess to serve. Society has lost faith in us except as image makers. It no longer believes we are working for the common good. In response, it has set up a maze of codes and lay-operated design review boards as a desperate defense against architects: architects they view either as obsessed with their own egos, or, more commonly, as the overly obedient servants of greedy and shortsighted clients. In California, even small neighborhoods now have review boards comprised of earnest but untrained laypeople instructing architects about window proportions, color, and internal circulation. Conflict is obligatory. Obviously, once a review board is in place, it has a responsibility to reject the architect's first design, no matter how skilled, since to accept it would imply impotence.

Review boards, of course, have been with the profession from the beginning (and architects have a long history of complaining about them). However, if in the past a review board was an occasional experience, now it is the norm. Worse, its focus now extends to details and artistic decisions long considered the exclusive domain of the architect.

The public's defensive and confrontational attitude is both logical and understandable—just look at the built environment. If we as architects claim expertise in this area, we also have to accept accountability for it. Yes, architects only design ten percent of built structures, moneylenders make the major design decisions, and construction managers now administer construction, but the state of the built landscape is still considered to be our fault. (The fact that we are blamed for all of this is encouraging—it implies that society still has a certain aspiration for us!)

Given the current state of professional practice, a responsible and caring architect has just three choices: quit, keep whining, or try to find a solution.

It seems to me there is a way to get back in sync or to find the fit.

The answer lies not in the architectural styles or polemics we find so entertaining, but in the way buildings are *made*—both the technical process of construction and the social process of design.

I have always been interested in using vernacular construction as a way to achieve fit with ever-decreasing project budgets. One can draw from two vernacular construction techniques in our region: light wood frame and tilt-up concrete slab. First seriously used by Irving Gill in the early part of this century, tilt-slab lay forgotten until warehouse builders discovered it with a vengeance in the 1960s. Although it has evolved to a highly sophisticated technical art, it is largely virgin territory for architects. Much of our recent work explores this utilitarian vernacular and its intriguing possibilities as a noble and even civic architecture.

Achieving a fit in the social process of design is even more critical. We must find a way to access the collective ego of those who are impacted by the buildings we design. In this area, fortunately, there is considerable precedent from which to draw. In the 1960s, Lawrence Halprin, Jim Burns, Charles Moore,

Environment: Shukugawa Demonstration House

Context: Case Study remodel

Technology: House for a musician

and others developed participatory methods for collective design. These models became popular for planning projects but have only occasionally been employed by architects for actual building design. Architects, fearing camels (horses designed by committee), are more comfortable with only token public participation in their art even though the ordeal of subsequent public confrontations eventually renders their design impotent.

In the 1960s collaborative design was a populist option. Today, it may be our only path toward gaining the artistic control that comes with confidence and respect. Once the collective ego is accessed, the art in architecture becomes the ability to create a single unified work—a single ego from a collective truth.

During this century we have focused on training artist-architects as museum artists. The results have been successful in the sense that the country is dotted with isolated examples of fine buildings. The costs, however, have been devastating and largely unintended.

Isolating art from its social context has produced architects viewed as superficial beautifiers. What educators see as an artist-architect capable of resolving complex problems for the benefit of society, the public sees as someone you call on to make things pretty. This is an artistic role, to be sure, but devoid of the substance that distinguishes architecture from decoration. Isolating the art of object-making from urban planning has contributed to the physical anarchy of our cities and suburbs. By emphasizing art as *the* goal, as opposed to an important by-product, we have degraded the architect's role from master builder to a specialist on the team and have given away our artistic authority. Pathetically, this is the very thing we are trained to attain. Architectural education has become essentially a sadistic enterprise: producing artist-architects for a role eliminated by the training itself.

To the purely service-oriented professional architect, this issue is not critical, as he or she gauges success on criteria other than artistic authority. The design elite—that small percentage of our profession that *has* attained authority as artist-architects—operates outside of normal social and economic constraints, serving "patron of the arts" clients. This group also takes little interest in these issues. In fact, they have every reason to endorse the system since it works to safeguard their status. That leaves the rest of us.

The academic institutions seem confused, misinterpreting the issue as "theory versus practice" or "intellectuals versus mechanics." It is not a question of producing draftspeople or principals, but rather of producing an architect with the skills to reclaim artistic authority in a socially meaningful way.

Solutions? There are many. The first has to do with teaching an attitude. Freshman students still arrive with unfortunate Ayn Rand fantasies from the 1940s. If a fine artist like Christo can find gratification not just in the objects he makes but also in the Byzantine process of permitting and constructing projects like *Running Fence*, then so can we.

In the same tradition that determines the antiquated zoning codes in our cities, educators think in terms of isolation rather than integration. How can structural concepts be taught outside the design studio as if they have nothing to do with the art of architecture? How can social and environmental concerns be considered a specialty?

Education also needs to distinguish between foreground architecture and background architecture. Students graduate without an appreciation of background architecture or an understanding of how to create it effectively. Because the educational system (and professional awards programs) does not value the incredible skills required to design an artful background, the built environment has become an anarchic assemblage of ego-driven foreground structures against a background left to less-skilled architects.

We must instill a system of values in which the art of architecture is more than schematic design, a system that teaches the importance of an integrated design process of multiple values, that considers skilled background work as important as foreground work, that portrays the user/community as collaborator rather than confrontational adversary.

We must focus on accessing
the collective rather than the individual ego –

then maybe we can effect the fit.

First printed in William S. Saunders, ed., *Reflections on Architectural Practices in the Nineties* (New York: Princeton Architectural Press, 1996), and first presented at a Harvard University Graduate School of Design Symposium in Spring 1991.

So she sat with closed eyes, and half believed herself in Wonderland,
though she knew she had but to open them again,
and all would change to dull reality.[1]

Southern California is an invention.

As if it were some vast real estate development, turn-of-the-century promoters and civic boosters packaged, scripted, and sold this arid, impoverished landscape as the manifestation of the Arcadian Dream.[2]

As Kevin Starr details in his social history of Southern California, the Arcadian Dream promised a better life by combining the best qualities of Anglo and Hispanic cultures. Yankee ingenuity and capitalistic skills,

An Architecture of 6

Rob Wellington Quigley

Contradictions

complemented by Latin graciousness and love of life, here would create a sun-drenched super society. Hand-colored chamber of commerce brochures from the turn of the century show hilarious juxtapositions of thriving industrial cities and bucolic orange groves. Distant, snow-capped mountains frame the scene, as a contented padre surveys the raging prosperity from the ruins of his arcaded mission.[3]

From the reality of a few crumbling mission outposts and several struggling ranchos, civic boosters concocted a rich, romantic history for Alta California.

"I do wonder what can have happened to me!
When I used to read fairy tales, I fancied that kind of thing never happened,
and now here I am in the middle of one!"

In many postindustrial incarnations, this myth of a new regional society is still with us today. An ambitious society that fills a cultural and historic void with invention instead of patient tradition may be unprecedented. Developers and civic groups ask for Spanish style. More sophisticated clients ask for less clichéd, more contemporary versions of the same.

In more established cultures, local traditions, the physical microclimate, and a clear sense of history combine to create a distinct architecture and sense of place. Short on both tradition and history, our mongrel society in Southern California was left to invent the Dream and abandon itself to the shortsighted expedience of twentieth-century capitalism. The resulting populist vernacular, with its graceful freeways, isolated convenience centers, and lack of public place, is largely a response to the advantages and limitations of the automobile.

Our vernacular has a life of its own. In its rare, pure state, untouched by architects trained in the art of "good taste" and shaped wholly by market forces, it has a certain perverse charm. The sculptural qualities of our better freeway interchanges are well-documented. Certain new low-end, tilt-up concrete slab warehouse districts seduce with a refreshing lack of pretense. The charm, however, usually remains unappreciated until plenty of time has passed. Imagine your grandchildren joining preservationist groups to save today's corner L-centers from twenty-first-century bulldozers!

Beyond this popular vernacular and the thinly picturesque imagery of the Arcadian Dream lie the issues that might define a more meaningful California regionalism today. They remain largely neglected by the architecture profession.

In a country that is fast minimizing the differences among cultures and regions, the search for a locally meaningful architecture is more and more relevant. Communication is becoming instantaneous, information universally available. Even regional speech patterns are coalescing into a bland monotone. Standardized graphics, franchised retail chains, and widely circulated architecture magazines further dissipate local identities. As the larger built environment shrinks and homogenizes, the need for architects to define the particular and to capture the spirit of the place becomes critical.

In Southern California, the keys to this spirit are contained in a series of colorful contradictions.

one

"I can't help it," said Alice very meekly; "I'm growing."
"You've no right to grow here," said the Dormouse.
"Don't talk nonsense," said Alice more boldly. "You know you're growing too."
"Yes, but I grow at a reasonable pace," said the Dormouse,
"not in that ridiculous fashion."

With Southern California population growth rates increasing exponentially, built environments are created almost instantly. The average Southern Californian stays put only a few years—a nomadic existence that adds to the

flux. Faced with this accelerating growth, people grasp for some notion of permanence, of stability.

Under these conditions the quick rise of nostalgic postmodernism and a longing for the symbols of a simpler time is understandable. And while today it may be more fashionable for architecture to celebrate transition and instability rather than nostalgia, the challenge is to create a contemporary architecture that reconciles the psychological need for permanence with the realities of a flexible, transient lifestyle.

two

"If everyone minded their own business,"
said the Duchess in a hoarse growl,
"the world would go round a deal faster than it does."

The nature of our public relationships is in the process of radical transformation. Ironically, new electronic means of communication and information-exchange leave us isolated. The rich subtleties and body language of face-to-face interaction have been replaced by the impersonal privacy of a modem and computer screen. Architects silently fax their dreams of active urban spaces and teeming sidewalk cafes to consultants just blocks away. City council meetings are televised and constituents vote by phone.

In a region where we spend much of our time alone in automobiles with car phones, and the rest sequestered in detached, single-family suburban houses, huddled around the TV set, what is the role of public urban space? How should architecture influence this contradiction of interactive isolation?

The solutions must create a built environment that uses the efficiency of the new communication devices and the luxury of instant information to enhance and promote real human interaction. A new intimacy may well be possible.

three

"You couldn't have it if you did want it,"
the Queen said. "The rule is, jam tomorrow
and jam yesterday—but never jam today."

Southern California abounds in political paradoxes. One of the most permissive and experimental regions in the United States is dominated by a morbid political conservatism. Orange County and most of San Diego County make small midwestern towns seem liberal. In the midst of the information revolution and new technologies that make possible low-cost publications, the massive populations of Los Angeles and San Diego are dominated by two monopolistic newspapers whose unchallenged views become truth. In a society that prides itself on free speech, we are, in fact, carefully managed by the media.

Architects deal with this irony daily. Clients see nothing unusual in urging the architect to do something new, original, and untried—as long as he or she avoids the unknown and the result looks like what was built last time. Marketing consultants carefully tabulate the responses to what has been built in the recent past. They take an average of the positive responses to this mediocrity and, in a breathtaking leap of logic, present it "scientifically" as the public's desire. Developers are mesmerized by the implied security of this process of formalized incest or product-inbreeding, even as their capitalist instincts argue for the new and innovative. Architect selection boards, often comprising very sophisticated people, avoid intelligent risks that individual members might otherwise take in an effort to be "responsible" to those they represent.

Besides seeing the humor in this, the challenge is to clarify these requests and distill them into a more honest and vibrant architecture. The danger lies in fearing the naked contradictions and trying to resolve them.

four

"But I don't want to go among mad people," Alice remarked.
"Oh, you can't help that," said the Cat. "We're all mad here. I'm mad. You're mad."
"How do you know I'm mad?" said Alice.
"You must be," said the Cat, "or you wouldn't have come here."

Coupled with the political paradox is a bizarre social paradox: Southern California is a region of laid-back high-achievers. Suntanned stockbrokers head for the office in their convertibles at 3:30 in the morning. High-stress meetings take place around the pool. One can imagine fax machines on executive skateboards and surfers breaking for power lunches. Casual and formal, driven and devil-may-care meet here every day.

The architect's challenge is to cling to the freedom and spontaneity possible in such a schizophrenic society. The danger lies in being swept up in the hedonism of instant gratification and momentary trends.

five

"Let the Looking-glass creatures, whatever they be,
Come and dine with the Red Queen, the White Queen, and me!"

Historically multicultural, Southern California architecture has, in the past, also acknowledged its Pacific Rim vantage point. Japanese design had a profound impact on the region in the early part of this century, as the evocative work of the Greene brothers filtered down to influence the bungalow court. Two generations of early Southern California modernists were also influenced by the calm clarity of traditional Japanese architecture. Mexican architecture and culture, of course, are central to the Dream.

These influences, however, were sanitized and stylized as they were incorporated into mass-produced housing: Southern California's more elite architects were largely concerned with only the formal issues of space and aesthetics.

As we become a less tidy, more diverse society, the challenge is to create an architecture that is sensitive not just to the subtlest of the region's cultural contributions. The relationship between Hispanic culture and the dominant Anglo culture is complex and rich with possibilities. Traditional melting pot notions are both limiting and inappropriate when, for some people, the mother country is only a few miles away.

In California, Anglos annexed the land and its people in the name of Manifest Destiny. More than 150 years have passed and the tensions still exist. Architecture must get beyond the romantic scenography of the Arcadian Dream and deal with a real relationship among cultures. The opportunity for a more meaningful built environment lies in promoting understanding and interaction among cultures while preserving and celebrating their distinct differences.

SIX

> Tweedledum looked round him with a satisfied smile.
> "I don't suppose," he said, "there'll be a tree left standing, for ever so far round,
> by the time we've finished!"

Physical forces give this region special character, but even an aspect as basic as our benign climate seems more bumbled than manipulated by local architects. We think of ecological awareness as a popular artifact from the 1960s. Despite the recurring crises of energy and resources, north arrows remain nothing more than a graphic symbol to most architects: buildings are routinely uninhabitable without air-conditioning and artificial light.

Honest concerns for the possible lifestyles our climate affords should lay the foundation for a distinct regional aesthetic. Perhaps dazzled by the Dream's promise of easy outdoor living, few architects design outdoor spaces as convenient, usable extensions of architectural space. Modification of glare, passive control of diurnal temperature swings, and manipulation of breezes seem virgin territory.

Our climate encourages experimentation with materials, and Southern California designers have risen to the challenge. Over the last few decades, snickers from cold-climate contemporaries have turned to respect and, ironically, emulation as local architects raised raw framing, cheap stucco, and asphalt shingles to an appropriately fragile art. At last, high art and a budget-driven, vernacular reality meet with inspired enthusiasm.

> It sounded an excellent plan, no doubt, and very neatly and simply arranged;
> the only difficulty was, that she had not the smallest idea how to set about it....
> "Would you tell me please how to get from here?"
> "That depends a good deal on where you want to get to."

In the face of these contradictions, how are today's Southern California architects to respond? Most have practiced as architectural pharmacists, mindlessly filling cosmetic prescriptions by the thousands. At the other extreme are those who simply negate the elusive regional issues altogether. Idiosyncratic personal concerns or the search for a universal or international aesthetic offer convenient sanctuaries. Modernist, postmodernist, or deconstructivist, the more global the solution, the less meaningful it is locally. But the reverse is not true. Only an authentically local architecture can transcend the provincial.

The best work of Southern California architects is tempered with concern for the more difficult aspects of regionalism. From the seminal Irving Gill and Rudolph Schindler to a calculated Richard Neutra and an intuitive Frank Gehry, these architects speak to a spirit and identity that are uniquely Southern Californian. The sensitive local focus of this work has given it importance and meaning far beyond this region.

It is the spirit rather than the visual identity that is the ultimate yardstick of regionalism. An experience rather than an object, an event rather than an artifact, the new regionalism I am concerned with will respond to the elusive contradictions outlined above. The new regionalism will be simple, yet painfully complex, knowingly unpretentious and casually sophisticated. At one with its brief history, it will evoke permanence through spirit and intellect rather than detail and nostalgia. Privacy must be be able to confront spontaneity and social accident. Pacific Rim and Hispanic cultures must be allowed to contribute their identities and local histories even as we work toward an "integrated" society.

In California a more authentic built environment can emerge from the struggle to weave an architecture of cultural diversity and contradiction. Comfortable only in its reaction to climate, the real Arcadian Dream will not be a blend, but a distinct, colorful collage of dislocation.

First printed in *Architecture California*, February 1991.

Locke House

1 Lewis Carroll, *Alice's Adventures in Wonderland* and *Through the Looking Glass* (New York: Simon & Schuster, 1982). All subsequent excerpts are from this edition.

2 See Kevin Starr, *California: Inventing the Dream* (New York: Oxford University Press, 1985).

3 Ibid.

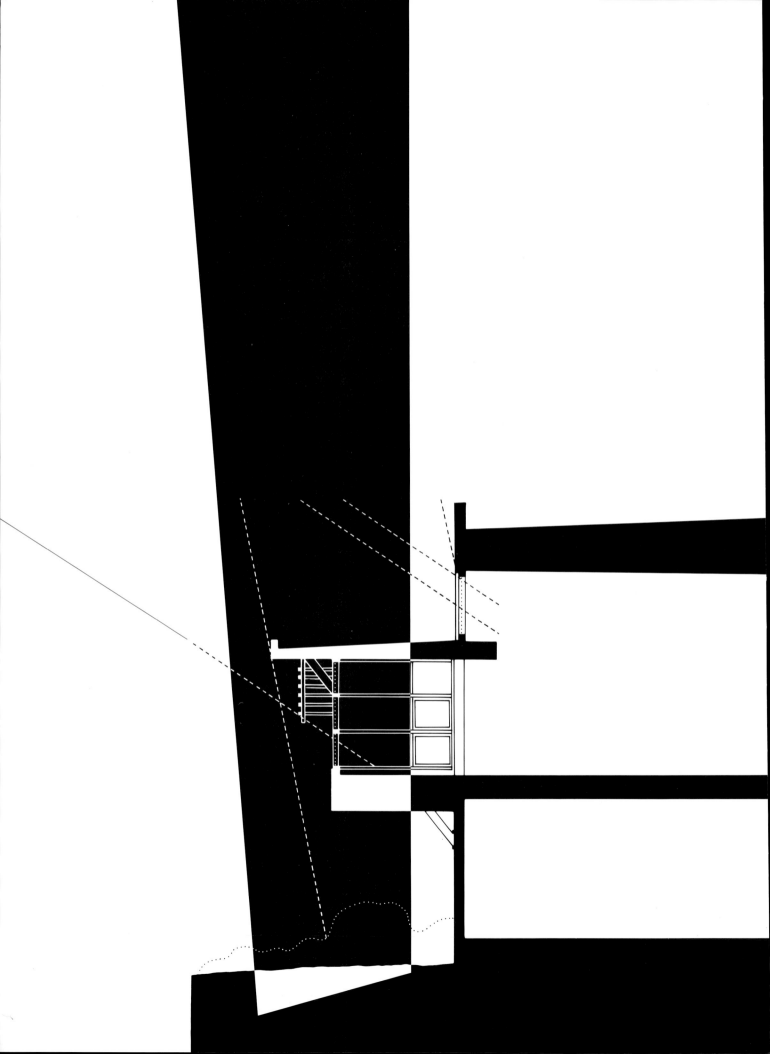

Books

Alves, Ronald, and Charles Milligan. ***Living with Energy.*** New York: Penguin Books, 1978

Betsky, Aaron. ***Violated Perfection: Architecture and the Fragmentation of the Modern.*** New York: Rizzoli International Publications, 1990

Davis, Sam. ***The Architecture of Affordable Housing.*** Berkeley: University of California Press, 1995

Gropp, Louis. ***Solar Houses.*** New York: Pantheon Books/Condé Nast Publications, 1978

Kemp, Jim. ***American Vernacular: Regional Influences in Architecture and Interior Design.*** Washington, D.C.: American Institute of Architects Press, 1990

Langdon, Philip. ***American Houses.*** New York: Stewart, Tabori & Chang, 1987

Larson, Magali Sarfatti. ***Behind the Postmodern Facade.*** New York: Princeton Architectural Press, 1993

Rieselbach, Anne, ed. ***Emerging Voices: A New Generation of Architects in America.*** New York: The Architectural League of New York and Princeton Architectural Press, 1986

Soloman, Daniel. ***ReBuilding.*** New York: Princeton Architectural Press, 1992

selected
bibliography
1974 – 1995

Magazines

1995
"Rob Wellington Quigley," *Architecture + Urbanism*, November 1995
"Neighborhood Hope," *Architecture*, June 1995

1994
"Capistrano Beach House," *GA Houses* 43, November 1994
"On the Boards: SRO Housing," *Architecture*, October 1994
"Designing for America's Children," *Architecture*, July 1994
"Low Cost Housing in the USA," *L'Industria Delle Costruzioni*, May 1994
"Developing SROs: A Low-Rent Housing Alternative," *Urban Land*, April 1994
"Beaumont Building," *GA Houses* 40, January 1994

1993
"Logements Sociaux à San Diego," *l'architecture d'aujourd'hui*, November 1993
"De Camelot a Sherwood," *La Cultura* (Spain), December 1993
"Tearing Down the Temple: The New Civic Architecture," *Architectural Record*, October 1993
"Viviendas Insomnes," *Arquitectura Viva* 31, July 1993
"A Small Room at the Inn," *Planning*, June 1993
"Project 1993," *GA Houses* 37, June 1993
"Celebrating Pluralism – Portfolio of 1993 AIA Honor Award Winners," *Architecture*, May 1993
"Ten Best Designs of 1992," *Time*, January 4, 1993
"Home Sweet Home," *Architecture*, January 1993

1992

"Crisis of Figuration in Contemporary Architecture," *Center: A Journal for Architecture in America,* vol. 7, Center for the Study of American Architecture, School of Architecture, University of Texas at Austin, 1992

"Rob Wellington Quigley: The Sanctuary and O'Hill Residences," *GA Houses* 34, 1992

"Town Nucleus," *Progressive Architecture,* December 1992

"Hotel California," *Architectural Review,* September 1992

"Island of Domesticity," *Architectural Record,* July 1992

"On the Boards: Private House," *Architecture,* February 1992

1991

"California Transit Stations," *Architecture,* September 1991

"The AD 100," *Architectural Digest,* August 1991

"Affordable Housing," *Progressive Architecture,* June 1991

"The Low Cost of Living," *Los Angeles Times Magazine,* January 6, 1991

1990

"Regional Transit," *Architectural Record,* September 1990

"Rob Wellington Quigley: Reed and Locke Residences," *GA Houses* 29, August 1990

"SRO Revival," *Architecture,* July 1990

"Only the Name of the Vines is French," *Hauser* (Germany), June 1990

"Rob Wellington Quigley: Capistrano Beach Glass House," *GA Houses* 28, April 1990

1989

"Places About Art, Places About Mind," *Landscape Architecture,* October 1989

"The New California Cottage," *House Beautiful,* September 1989

"Locke Residence," *Nikkei Architecture* (Japan), September 1989

"Outpost of Civility," *Architectural Record,* April 1989

1988

"New Civic Center," *Progressive Architecture,* November 1988

"Solving the Housing Crisis," *Progressive Architecture,* October 1988

"New Mission: Learning from San Diego," *Metropolitan Home,* July 1988

"Help for the Homeless," *Newsweek,* April 11, 1988

"Rob Wellington Quigley: Kaplan Residence," *GA Houses* 22, January 1988

1987

"Architecture as Dance," *San Diego Home/Garden,* October 1987

"After Arcadia," *Architectural Record,* June 1987

"Olympic Park Project," *American Urbanism* (Japan), June 1987

"Rob Wellington Quigley: Monahan Residence and Jaeger Beach House," *GA Houses* 21, January 1987

1986

"Civic Projects by 40 Under 40 Designers Lead to Interiors Business," *Interiors,* December 1986

"40 Under 40," *Interiors,* September 1986

"Architecture: Rob Wellington Quigley," *Architectural Digest,* August 1986

"Palmy Days in San Diego," *Architectural Record,* March 1986

"Southern California Interiors," *L.A. Architect,* March 1986

"In Progress: Marina Palms Apartments," *Progressive Architecture,* February 1986

1985

"Rob Wellington Quigley," *Interiors,* September 1985

"The Reign of Spain – Mediterranean Revival," *Arts & Architecture,* July 1985

"Architecture: Rob Wellington Quigley," *Architectural Digest* (Japan), March 1985

"G Street Mole Embarcadero," *Center: Architecture for the Emerging City,* vol. 1, Center for the Study of American Architecture, School of Architecture, University of Texas at Austin, 1985

"Rob Wellington Quigley: Pacifica Condominiums," *GA Houses* 17, January 1985

1984

"The 1984 Register: An Explosion of Creators," *Esquire*, December 1984

"Architettura: Rob Wellington Quigley," *Architectural Digest* (Italy), November 1984

"Contemporary Art and Architecture," *Arts & Architecture*, Autumn 1984

"Three San Diego Architects," *GA Houses* 16, September 1984

"Eden in Salotto," *Ville Giardini* (Italy), September 1984

"Architecture: Rob Wellington Quigley," *Architectural Digest*, May 1984

"House for a Musician," *Architectural Record*, May 1984

"Pacifica Townhomes," *Progressive Architecture*, January 1984

"New Designs from Rob Quigley's Office," *Our House* (Japan), January 1984

1983

"Restaurants as Theater," *Arts & Architecture*, June 1983

"In Progress: Jaeger Residence," *Progressive Architecture*, April 1983

"Complex of Passive Function," *Kenchiku Bunka* (Japan), April 1983

1982

"The California Condition," *Architecture California*, November 1982

"Found Folie," *Progressive Architecture*, August 1982

"Sulla Baia di San Diego," *Abitare*, May 1982

"Fiesta Park," *L.A. Architect*, April 1982

"SoCal NoCal," *Progressive Architecture*, March 1982

1981

"Shukugawa Demonstration House," *Nikkei Architecture* (Japan), December 1981

"California 101," *Arts & Architecture*, Fall 1981

"Interview: Rob Quigley," *Architecture California*, October 1981

"Una Casa per La Musica," and **"Un Nuovo Quartiere-Villagio,"** *Abitare*, October 1981

"Shukugawa Demonstration House," *Sinzyutaka* (Japan), September 1981

"Shukugawa Demonstration House," *Kenchiku Bunka* (Japan), August 1981

"Shaped by the Sun," *Los Angeles Times Home*, February 8, 1981

1980

"Squire House," *Process Architecture* 21 (Japan), Winter 1980

"Cohen Residence, Squire Residence," *Architecture + Urbanism*, August 1980

"Un Percorso Americano," *Abitare*, June 1980

1979

"Una Forma per Il Sole," *Abitare*, December 1979

"Das Traumland und Seine Luxuhauser: Californien," *Architektur und Wohnen*, February 1979

1978

"Negli USA: Casa Solare," *Ville Giardini* (Italy), September 1978

1977

"Residential Energy – Conserving Design," *Los Angeles Architect*, December 1977

"A Theater for Living," *Los Angeles Times Home*, July 24, 1977

1974

"A Great Leap Forward," *San Diego Magazine*, August 1974

Honors
and Awards

Honors and Recognition

Firm Award, AIA California Council, 1995

Tau Sigma Delta Silver Medal, Texas Tech University, College of Architecture, 1994

Distinguished Alumnus Award, University of Utah, 1993

Elected **Associate Member of the National Academy of Design,** 1993

Included in **"Ten Best Designs of 1992,"** *Time* magazine,
for the design of 202 Island Inn, 1993

Elected **Fellow of the American Institute of Architects,** 1991

Included in **"The AD 100,"** *Architectural Digest*, September 1991

Presidential Commendation for Exemplary Community Service,
for the design of the Baltic Inn, 1988

Selected for **"Forty Under Forty,"** The Architectural League of New York, 1986

Included in **"The Best of the New Generation: Men and Women Under Forty
Who Are Changing America,"** *Esquire*, 1984 Register

Museum & Gallery Exhibits

"Recent Work," University of Utah, March 1993

"10 Californian Architects," Royal Institute of British Architects, London, July 1992

"Faculty Exhibit," University of California at San Diego, September 1992

**"The Experimental Tradition: Twenty-Five Years of American
Architecture Competition,"** The Architectural League of New York, 1992

"Recent Work," University of Utah, January 1992

"Recent Work," solo exhibition, Portland State University, November 1991

"Housing Environments: A Cross Cultural Perspective," University of California at
San Diego, May 1991

"An Architecture of Substance: Farm Structures to Contemporary Houses,"
Brunnier Gallery and Museum, Iowa State University, 1990

"Five Choose Five," National AIA Conference, St. Louis, 1989, curated by Charles Moore

"The Emerging Generation in the USA," Global Architecture Gallery,
Tokyo, Japan, November 1987

"Unbuilt Architecture," Grace Design, Houston, Texas, Summer 1986
(traveling exhibition 1986 to 1989)

"Beaumont Building," solo exhibition, La Jolla Museum of Contemporary Art,
February 1985

"G Street Mole," California Polytechnic State University, San Luis Obispo, February 1985

"Don Clos Pegase Competition," San Francisco Museum of Modern Art,
July 1985

"Exhibit of Recent Work," solo exhibition, University of California at
Los Angeles, November 1984

"At Home with Architecture," Mandeville Gallery, University of California at
San Diego, February 1983

"California Condition," La Jolla Museum of Contemporary Art,
curated by Stanley Tigerman, November 1982

"Visual Communication Towards Architecture," Installation Gallery,
San Diego, August 1982

"Retrospective," solo exhibition, Southern California Institute of Architecture,
Santa Monica, April 1982

Faculty Positions

University of California at San Diego, Graduate School of Architecture, Adjunct Professor, 1990 to present
University of California at Berkeley, Visiting Instructor, Fall 1994
University of Texas at Austin, Visiting Instructor, Spring 1994
Catholic University of America, Washington, D.C., Visiting Critic, 1993
La Universidad Autonoma de Baja California, Mexico, Visiting Instructor, 1993
Harvard University Graduate School of Design, Visiting Design Critic, Spring 1991
Arizona State University, Department of Architecture, Visiting Instructor, Fall 1990
University of Pennsylvania, Department of Architecture, Graduate Design Studio, Visiting Instructor, Fall 1988
University of California at Los Angeles, Department of Architecture, Graduate Design Studio,
Visiting Instructor, Spring 1982
University of Southern California, Department of Architecture, Lecturer in Environmental Technology, Spring 1980
University of California at San Diego, Extension Division, Instructor of Environmental Design, 1976, 1977

Awards

National AIA Awards

AIA Honor Award, 1993
202 Island Inn

AIA California Council Awards

AIA Firm Award, 1995

AIA Honor Award
with Distinction, 1994
202 Island Inn

AIA Honor Award, 1994
Foreston Trends Corporate
Headquarters and Warehouse

AIA Honor Award, 1993
La Pensione at India & Date

AIA Honor Award, 1993
Tustin Ranch Clubhouse
and Community Center

AIA Honor Award, 1991
J Street Inn

People in Architecture Award,
1991
J Street Inn

AIA Honor Award, 1989
Linda Vista Library

AIA Honor Award, 1985
Video Porch, La Jolla Museum of
Contemporary Art

AIA Honor Award, 1985
Oxley Residence

California Regional AIA Awards

AIA Citation, Pasadena/ Foothill
Chapter, 1990
Brea by Design –
The Downtown Charrette

AIA Design Award, Los Angeles
Chapter, 1981
QBM Building

San Diego AIA Awards

AIA Merit Award, 1985
Foreston Trends Corporate
Headquarters and Warehouse

AIA Citation, 1994
Capistrano Beach Glass House

AIA Merit Award, 1993
St. David's Episcopal Church

AIA Merit Award, 1993
202 Island Inn

AIA Certificate of Recognition, 1993
La Pensione at India & Date

AIA Certificate of Recognition,
Divine Detail, 1993
Courtyard Fountain, La Pensione
at India & Date

AIA Certificate of Recognition,
Divine Detail, 1993
Capistrano Beach Glass House

AIA Merit Award, 1992
University of Nevada at Las Vegas,
School of Architecture

AIA Citation, 1992
Malibu Studio Hotel

AIA Merit Award, 1991
Tustin Ranch Clubhouse
and Community Center

AIA Merit Award, 1991
La Pensione at India & Date

AIA Citation, Divine Detail, 1991
Reed House

AIA Honor Award, 1990
J Street Inn

AIA Citation, 1990
Escondido Transit Center

AIA Citation, 1990
Beaumont Building

AIA Citation, 1990
Sherman Heights Community Center

AIA Citation, Divine Detail, 1990
Linda Vista Library

AIA Merit Award, 1989
Tustin Ranch Clubhouse and
Community Center

AIA Merit Award, 1988
Linda Vista Library

AIA Merit Award, 1988
Locke House

AIA Honor Award, 1987
Baltic Inn

AIA Honor Award, 1987
Miraflores

AIA Honor Award, 1987
Monahan House

AIA Citation, 1986
Coronado Design Guidelines

AIA Honor Award, 1985
Jaeger Beach House

AIA Merit Award, 1985
Video Porch, La Jolla Museum
of Contemporary Art

AIA Merit Award, 1985
600 Front Street Apartments

AIA Merit Award, 1985
Beaumont Building

AIA Citation, 1985
Cathedrangel

AIA Honor Award, 1984
House for a Musician

AIA Honor Award, 1984
Oxley House

AIA Honor Award, 1984
Pacific Wine Bar

AIA Merit Award, 1983
Sterrett House

AIA Citation, 1983
Jaeger Beach House

AIA Merit Award, 1982
Shukugawa Demonstration House

AIA Citation, 1982
QBM Building

AIA Merit Award, 1982
Forecast 80's

AIA Citation, 1982
Fiesta Park Condominiums

AIA Honor Award, 1981
Sayer Beach House

AIA Merit Award, 1981
Case Study Remodel

AIA Merit Award, 1979
Squire House

AIA Honor Award, 1976
Cohen House

List of Buildings and Projects

Public Buildings

Early Childhood Education Center, University of California at San Diego, 1995
Solana Beach Transit Station, Solana Beach, CA, 1995
Balboa Park Activity Center, San Diego, 1996 (with Wheeler Wimer Blackman & Associates)
Sherman Heights Community Center, San Diego, 1994
Tustin Ranch Clubhouse and Community Center, Tustin, CA, 1990
Tijuana River Estuary Visitor Center, Imperial Beach, CA, 1990
Escondido Transit Center, Escondido, CA, 1990
Linda Vista Library, San Diego, 1987
Carlsbad City Hall Remodel, Carlsbad, CA, 1987
Video Porch, La Jolla Museum of Contemporary Art, La Jolla, CA, 1984
San Diego Municipal Gymnasium, San Diego (project/with Wheeler Wimer Blackman & Associates)
University of Nevada at Las Vegas, School of Architecture, Las Vegas, NV (project)
Mesa College Art Gallery/Museum, San Diego (project)
Energy Efficient State Office Building, Sacramento, CA (project)

Single Room Occupancy Hotels

Alma Place, Palo Alto, CA, 1996
202 Island Inn, San Diego, 1992
La Pensione at India & Date, San Diego, 1991
J Street Inn, San Diego, 1990
Baltic Inn, San Diego, 1987
Malibu Studio Hotel, San Diego (project)
Huntington Beach SRO, Huntington Beach, CA (project)
919 The Alameda, San Jose, CA (project)

Mixed-Use Projects

Solana Beach Retail and Housing, Solana Beach, CA, 1996
Del Prado Apartments, Los Angeles, 1992 (urban design)
Beaumont Building, San Diego, 1988
Don Pico Apartments and Retail, San Diego, 1988
QBM Building, Palos Verdes, CA, 1980
Catellus Mixed-Use Development, Oceanside, CA (project)
Park & University Mixed-Use Project, San Diego (project)
La Entrada, San Diego (project)
G Street Mole, San Diego (project)
Birtcher Mixed-Use Development, Del Mar, CA (project)

Retail/Industrial

Foreston Trends Corporate Headquarters and Warehouse, Long Beach, CA, 1994
Village Hat Shop, San Diego, 1986
Windsor Industrial Park, Santa Rosa, CA, 1985
Pacific Wine Bar, San Diego, 1982
The Bookmark, San Diego (project)

Places of Worship

St. David's Episcopal Church, San Diego, 1996
Unitarian Universalist Fellowship of San Dieguito, Solana Beach, CA, 1996

Medical Facilities

Child Life Center, Torrance, CA, 1985
Escondido Surgery Center, Escondido, CA, 1985

Multi-Family Housing

Shaw Lopez Ridge, San Diego, 1996
Camino Real Townhomes, Del Mar, CA, 1995
Esperanza Garden Apartments, Solana Beach, CA, 1994 (with Salerno/Livingston Architects)
600 Front Street Apartments, San Diego, 1988
Forecast 80's, San Diego, 1984
Oliver Street Homes, San Diego, 1983
Pacifica Townhomes, San Diego, 1980
Houlihan Palms, San Diego, 1978
Ocean Beach Apartments, San Diego, 1973
M. F. & Ace Co. Building, San Diego (project)
Fiesta Park Apartments, Brawley, CA (project)

Single Family Houses

Alden House, Beverly Hills, CA, 1996
Capistrano Beach Glass House, Capistrano Beach, CA, 1993
The Sanctuary, Telluride, CO, 1992
Reed House, San Diego, 1989
Alden House, Pacific Palisades Highlands, CA, 1988
Locke House, Temecula, CA, 1987
Valkirs House, Escondido, CA, 1987
Kaplan House, Del Mar, CA, 1986
Miraflores, Rancho Santa Fe, CA, 1986
Monahan House, La Jolla, CA, 1986
OB Del, San Diego, 1986
Asche House, Coronado, CA, 1985
Cowan House, Soquel, CA, 1985
Cox House, Coronado, CA, 1984
Ray's House, Palos Verdes, CA, 1984
Pankey House, Bonsall, CA, 1984
Oxley House, La Jolla, CA, 1983
Jaeger Beach House, Del Mar, CA, 1983
Sterrett House, Rancho Santa Fe, CA, 1983
Jenkins House, Pauma Valley, CA, 1982
Shukugawa Demonstration House, Osaka, Japan, 1981
House for a Musician, San Diego, 1981
Sayer Beach House, San Diego, 1980
Case Study Remodel, Del Mar, CA, 1980
Johnson House, San Diego, 1980
Houlihan House, San Diego, 1979
Gudmundson House, San Diego, 1979
Squire House, Del Mar, CA, 1978
Solar House, Sherman Oaks, CA, 1978
Cohen House, Del Mar, CA, 1975
Seapy House, Fallbrook, CA, 1975
Barszewski House, Palos Verdes, CA, 1975
Gudmundson House, Del Mar, CA, 1974
Vivrette House, Laguna Beach, CA, 1973

Planning Projects

Tanforan/BART Concept Plan, San Bruno, CA, 1995
South Scripps Neighborhood Design Guidelines, University of California at San Diego, 1995 (with Wallace Roberts & Todd)
Fontana Civic Center Design Charette, Fontana, CA, 1990
Ocean Beach Beachfront Master Plan, San Diego, 1989
Brea by Design, Brea, CA, 1989
Vista Downtown Plan, Vista, CA, 1988
Newport Avenue Commercial Improvement Program, San Diego, 1987
El Cajon Boulevard Design Guidelines, San Diego, 1985 (with Land Studio)
Imperial Beach Beachfront Master Plan, Imperial Beach, CA, 1984
Coronado Design Guidelines, Coronado, CA, 1984
Del Mar 2000, Del Mar, CA, 1982

Office Staff 1978–1995

1995
Bob Dickens
Guillermo Tomaszewski
Catherine Herbst
Maryanne Welton

Leslie Marino

Wendell Shackelford
Roberta Aldrich
Todd Rinehart
George Hideg
Celso Gonzalez
Duncan MacIntosh
Scot Bennett

1994
Bob Dickens
Guillermo Tomaszewski
Catherine Herbst
Maryanne Welton

Leslie Marino

Wendell Shackelford
Roberta Aldrich
Todd Rinehart
Teddy Cruz
George Hideg

1993
Bob Dickens
Guillermo Tomaszewski
John Silber
Catherine Herbst

Maryanne Welton

Wendell Shackelford
Roberta Aldrich
Todd Rinehart
Teddy Cruz
Kate Roe
George Hideg

1992
Bob Dickens
Guillermo Tomaszewski
John Silber
Catherine Herbst

Maryanne Welton

Wendell Shackelford
Roberta Aldrich
Todd Rinehart
Kate Roe

1991
Bob Dickens
Guillermo Tomaszewski
Bill Behun
John Silber

Maryanne Welton

Teddy Cruz
Julie Scaramella
Wendell Shackelford
Catherine Herbst
Roberta Aldrich

1990
Bob Dickens
Guillermo Tomaszewski
Bill Behun
John Silber

Maryanne Welton

Judy Clinton
Helen Ewing
Kevin Freitas
Teddy Cruz
Colin Parmalee
Julie Scaramella
Wendell Shackelford
Catherine Herbst
Roberta Aldrich

1989
Bob Dickens
Guillermo Tomaszewski
Bill Behun

Maryanne Welton

Judy Clinton
Michael Golino
Todd Jager
Loralee Arnold
Helen Ewing
Kevin Freitas
Teddy Cruz
Colin Parmalee
Julie Scaramella
Catherine Herbst
David Dahlberg

1988
Bob Dickens
Mel McGee
Guillermo Tomaszewski
Bill Behun

Maryanne Welton

Judy Clinton
Michael Golino
Todd Jager
Loralee Arnold
Sheri Hirsch
Helen Ewing
Kevin Freitas

1987
Bob Dickens
Mel McGee
Guillermo Tomaszewski
Bill Behun

Maryanne Welton

Bruno Duarte
Judy Clinton
Michael Golino
Todd Jager
Loralee Arnold
Sheri Hirsch

1986
Bob Dickens
Mel McGee
Guillermo Tomaszewski
Bill Behun
Vladimir Frank

Maryanne Welton

Bruno Duarte
Judy Clinton
Kathleen Hallahan
Michael Golino
Terrie Long
Todd Jager

1985
Bob Dickens
Mel McGee
Guillermo Tomaszewski
Bill Behun
Vladimir Frank

Maryanne Welton

Bruno Duarte
Judy Clinton
Kathleen Hallahan
Michael Golino
Terrie Long

1984
Bob Dickens
Mel McGee
Herb Lira
Guillermo Tomaszewski
Bill Behun

Maryanne Welton

Bruno Duarte
Jackie Geller
Dorie White
Jackie Herman

1983
Bob Dickens
Mel McGee
Herb Lira

Maryanne Welton

Martin Sprouse
Trudy Morse Verdick
Bruno Duarte
Jackie Geller
Dorie White

1982
Bob Dickens
Bill Behun

Maryanne Welton

Mel McGee
Martin Sprouse

1981
Bob Dickens
Bill Behun

Maryanne Welton

Mel McGee
Martin Sprouse
Mario Lara

1980
Bob Dickens
Bill Behun
Jack Mosher

Maryanne Welton

Mel McGee
Trudy Morse Verdick

1979
Bob Dickens
Bill Behun
Jack Mosher
Lee Platt

Maryanne Welton

Mel McGee
Trudy Morse Verdick
Kathleen Hallahan

1978
Bob Dickens
Bill Behun
Jack Mosher
Lee Platt

Maryanne Welton

Mel McGee
Trudy Morse Verdick
Gary Paige

Credits

Collaborators

Adams Design Group, landscape architecture, pages 16, 90, 126

Marlo Bartels, tile artist, page 46

Ed Carpenter, glass artist, page 46

Raul Guerrero, artist, page 50

Mary Kuhnen, interior design, page 78

Land Studio, landscape architecture, page 62

Christopher Lee, artist, page 46

Kathleen McCormick, colorist, all projects

McCulley Design Group, interior and signage design, pages 16, 30, 40, 114, 132, 136

Marum Associates ASLA, landscape architecture, page 72

Patrick Quigley & Associates, lighting design, all projects

Raymond L. Quigley, conceptual engineering, all projects

Salerno/Livingston Architects, page 126

Andrew Spurlock Martin Poirier Landscape Architects, pages 50, 100, 106, 114, 132, 136, 178

Wheeler Wimer Blackman & Associates, pages 100, 178

Photographs

© **Michael Arthur,** page 88

© **Richard Barnes,** pages 17-29

© **Bill Behun,** page 78

© **Kim Brun,** pages 161-163

© **Jim Coit,** page 221

© **Glenn Cormier,** pages 113, 115, 119

© **Frank Domin,** pages 63, 66-71

© **Catherine Herbst,** page 51

© **David Hewitt/Anne Garrison,** cover, pages 4, 9, 31, 36, 40, 44, 49, 50, 53, 60, 73, 77, 80-83, 117, 121, 123, 124, 127, 128, 131, 133, 135-137, 139-141, 147, 193, 194, 202

© **Milroy/McAleer,** page 84

© **Arthur Ollman,** pages 144, 145

© **Rob Quigley,** pages 2, 10, 12, 13, 15, 30, 32-34, 37, 39, 41-43, 45-47, 51, 52, 54, 56-59, 61, 65, 74, 75, 79, 81, 85, 90, 92, 99, 118, 120, 122, 125, 129, 132, 134, 137, 143, 146, 149, 152-160, 183, 189, 190, 192, 196, 198-200, 203, 211

© **Kate Roe,** page 96

© **Stephen Simpson,** page 38

© **Toshi Yoshimi,** pages 87, 89, 195

Drawings

Jay Andrews, pages 167, 168, 171, 172, 173

Teddy Cruz, pages 22, 27, 31, 35, 39, 46, 55, 57, 60, 75, 80, 106-108, 110, 111, 119, 124, 134, 142, 150, 151, 155, 176, 178, 179, 181, 184-187

Bob Dickens, pages 46, 86, 98, 166, 167, 170, 173-175, 183

Bruno Duarte, page 63

Kevin Freitas, page 72

Celso Gonzalez, pages 44, 100, 217

Jim McCarthy, pages 93, 97, 99

Mel McGee, pages 170, 174, 175

Rob Quigley, pages 47, 109, 114, 126, 138, 160

Todd Rinehart, pages 94-96, 101, 103, 111, 123, 127, 130, 180, 182, 183

Wendell Shackelford, pages 11, 24, 42, 51, 64, 67, 91, 98, 99, 102, 111, 118, 129, 130, 163